The American church is in crisis today because of rampant moral failure, and too few leaders have had the courage or the wisdom to solve this dilemma. I am thankful that Larry Stockstill has written this important book. Finally someone has brought sanity to the contentious issue of biblical restoration. Like a skilled physician, Larry has diagnosed the problem and given us a clear remedy that is 100 percent biblical. I recommend this book to all leaders as well as to all Christians who have been affected by moral crisis in the church.

—J. Lee Grady
Editor, *Charisma* magazine

Larry Stockstill echoes a heartfelt concern that I've had for some time. Ministers and church leaders desperately need a call to repentance and spiritual refreshing. I sense Larry's desire is to offer ministers who may be experiencing personal defeat the opportunity to find help and hope without the fear of being shamed by others for what they may be personally ashamed of. Ministers have found it difficult to discover expressions of unconditional love toward them, as demonstrated by the father of the prodigal. Larry isn't simply pointing out a problem; he is seeking to offer help to those who hurt and experience defeat, including church leaders. I think this book is critically important for the health of the whole church.

—James Robison
President and Founder
LIFE Outreach International
Fort Worth, Texas

The church, led by pastors, is the spiritual conscience of our nation. But how can the church be the conscience if its credibility is in question because of compromise? Brother Larry Stockstill has a message for our nation's leaders that is urgently needed. We must demand greater personal accountability of ourselves as leaders in both the pulpit and in politics.

—TONY PERKINS
PRESIDENT, FAMILY RESEARCH COUNCIL

The Holy Spirit is laying the grounds for a new awakening in American Christianity. This book, I believe, is part of His strategy. We've been fed husks for too long, dressed them with sauces named "style, guide-growth, self-recognition, and media success," and a famine of true righteousness and wisdom and the desirable fruit they bring has resulted. Join me in opening your mind as a leader and servant of Christ to this sensitive and sensible call— issued with passion and love without self-righteousness.

—JACK W. HAYFORD
PRESIDENT, THE FOURSQUARE CHURCH
CHANCELLOR, THE KING'S COLLEGE & SEMINARY

The REMNANT

The
REMNANT

LARRY
STOCKSTILL

Charisma
HOUSE
A Strang Company

THE REMNANT by Larry Stockstill
Published by Charisma House
A Strang Company
600 Rinehart Road
Lake Mary, Florida 32746
www.strangdirect.com

Design Director: Bill Johnson
Cover design by Tracy Guillory, Judith Wright
Cover Images: © iStock, Photographer Chris Burt

Library of Congress Cataloging-in-Publication Data

Stockstill, Larry, 1953-
  The remnant / Larry Stockstill.
     p. cm.
  Includes bibliographical references (p.   ).
  ISBN 978-1-59979-454-9
 1. Church renewal--United States. 2. Evangelicalism--United States.
 3. United States--Moral conditions. I. Title.
  BV600.3.S75 2008
  262.001'7--dc22
  2008027853

08 09 10 11 12 — 9 8 7 6 5 4 3 2
Printed in the United States of America

CONTENTS

Preface xi

Part 1: Help for the Dysfunctional Church

Chapter 1: Mentoring for the Unfathered Church....................1

Chapter 2: Standards for the Uncorrected Church 12

Chapter 3: Multiplication for the Unfruitful Church.............19

Chapter 4: Healing for the Unhealed Church..........................27

Chapter 5: The Scriptures for the Untaught Church............. 38

Part 2: The Ten Commandments of Ministry

Chapter 6: Commandment 1: Prayer 49

Chapter 7: Commandment 2: Bible Study 59

Chapter 8: Commandment 3: Integrity.....................................70

Chapter 9: Commandment 4: Purity 83

Chapter 10: Commandment 5: Example................................. 100

Chapter 11: Commandment 6: Relationships 114

Chapter 12: Commandment 7: Philosophy............................. 128

Chapter 13: Commandment 8: Faith 142

Chapter 14: Commandment 9: Spiritual Warfare................ 154

Chapter 15: Commandment 10: Wisdom.............................. 164

Epilogue: A Personal Code of Conduct 178

Notes..181

PREFACE

I'M GOING TO SHAKE THIS NATION. THE WORDS thundered into my spirit on an airplane somewhere over Oklahoma. It was the first week of October 2006, and I was en route from speaking that morning in Louisville to another speaking engagement that evening in Dallas. I was a bit tired, having left Baton Rouge that morning, and was really not expecting any type of message from the Lord at that moment.

When I returned home that evening, the Lord spoke to me again about His promised shaking, that it would begin with the body of Christ and would be unlike anything we had ever experienced before. I asked the Lord to begin by shaking me, waking me out of my own lethargy and sleep. I then shared this word with a small group of pastors I meet with monthly in Baton Rouge for fellowship and accountability. Finally, I preached on it that weekend at our church, Bethany World Prayer Center, where I have been pastoring for almost twenty-five years. We all took the challenge to allow the Lord to stir the smoldering coals of our hearts and awaken us from the stupor of apathy.

True to His word, the Lord, indeed, did begin a major cleansing in His house. Ministry after ministry came under direct scrutiny and fire for sexual immorality, financial impropriety, skewed doctrine, lavish lifestyles, and countless other issues, both small and great. The body of Christ—His representation on Earth, His ambassador, His *bride*—flaunted soiled garments for all to see and the gleeful world to ridicule.

As painful as God's shaking has been (and will continue to be), it has awakened a new breed of pastors and laypeople alike who will ask the tough questions: Where has the glory gone (God's glory, that is) in the American church? When did we make the shift from laying it all down for the sake of Christ to joining the latest "bless me" club? When did the simple, pure gospel of the Savior become about "me," "my," and "mine"? What happened to the *transparency* and *integrity* that marked the church for centuries, when following Christ meant hardship, denial, and even death?

Transparency and *integrity*. Those two words haven't been used in quite some time to describe the American church. By God's grace, however, we are going to change that. That is why you are holding this book. I believe the Lord led you to it and is calling you to become part of a new breed of Christians— a remnant—who will follow Him with both transparency and integrity.

With all of the public exposure of so many ministries, I am now more convinced than ever that God's judgment is imminent upon our nation. Early last year, James Robison from Dallas contacted me and encouraged me to read his article "Warning to America." He senses that we as a nation are moving toward either *humility* or *humiliation*. Our secret sins have brought us to a moment where God is ready to shake our nation in radical ways. James proposes that if we do not humble ourselves and repent, we could become a third-world nation living without electricity or running water. On the phone that day, we agreed that although all Christians must be bastions of integrity, the pastors of America are the key to stopping an awful judgment that is looming on the horizon of our great nation.

Do we realize how precipitous is our position as a nation? The world financial markets are spiraling downward. Rogue nations are going nuclear and possibly proliferating their weapons to others. Terrorists are constructing endless plots to wreak havoc in our safe cities. We feel secure, but even secular programs show us that we are one blast, one germ, one market turn away from collapse as a nation.

It is for that purpose I am writing this book. There are currently about 380,000 churches in America, all of them pastored by someone. And not one of those pastors is immune to the enemy's subtle attack. We must now ask the question, what percentage of America's spiritual leaders are living a double life? I asked another high-profile leader who deals with thousands of pastors what his guess would be, and he said, "Perhaps 20 percent."

That is 75,000 leaders in trouble. We certainly have no authority to speak to Washington, Hollywood, and New York about morality and ethics in our families and relationships if we are leading double lives beset with addictions, perversion, divorce, and questionable financial practices.

And if the problem is this great in the ministry, what must it be like for those we are trying to lead? What hidden struggles are they wrestling with? How many of them are showing up in our churches on Sunday with smiles on their faces to mask the desperation that engulfs them Monday through Saturday?

We know that America has some wonderful, committed, holy leaders and believers. Perhaps you are one of them. In Ezekiel's vision, the man dressed in linen placed a mark on the forehead of those who "sigh and groan over all the abominations that are committed in it [Jerusalem]" (Ezek. 9:4, RSV). I believe there is a righteous remnant of godly pastors and believers who grieve for the direction of the American church.

However, the question becomes, how much longer will God tolerate our duplicity? It is amazing to me that as our churches grow larger, our nation seemingly grows darker morally. The church seems obsessed with growth and "relating" to America, but it reminds me of Samson before his haircut. Though engaged in immorality, Samson continued to function in his gift for years, but he no longer carried his anointing.

How can an individual continue to grow a huge church or ministry and yet be struggling with secret sin? The answer is simple: a person's gift will make room for him and attract the notice and attention of others. Furthermore, that gift, though legitimate and God given, can be operated in pride and arrogance rather than in submission to God. This was Satan's problem: *unbroken, unyielded giftings.*

In the church world, education, connections, manipulation, innovation, entrepreneurship, and aggressiveness can amplify a person's gift. The fact that someone's ministry continues to expand and looks exciting is no guarantee that the person is operating in the *anointing.*

The anointing operates in brokenness and is yielded at the cross. The anointing focuses people on Jesus instead of a person. It is "pure, then peaceable, gentle, willing to yield, full of mercy and good fruits, without partiality and without hypocrisy" (James 3:17, NKJV). The anointing submits to the correction of others, is transparent, and operates in relaxation and peace.

When we begin to force ourselves, assert ourselves, and promote ourselves, we are moving in our gifting. Unless we daily bring our giftedness to the cross and allow it to be broken, we can easily move into the pride and curse that Satan suffered in heaven.

God is calling for change. Every day our newspapers relate the stories of what we thought were exemplary ministries announcing the amicable divorce of their leaders or a violent end to their marriage. Conservative, pro-family political leaders face public humiliation when their names appear on a prostitute's phone list or a policeman catches them in a compromised position in a restroom.

Pastors divorce their wives, marry assistants, sell church properties, and simply start other churches elsewhere. Huge mainline denominations as well as independent churches are reeling from the impact of the exposures of so many fallen leaders. We must do something radical and immediate. The patient is internally bleeding, though perfect in outward health and appearance.

I challenge you to carefully consider the thoughts, trends, and principles the Lord has taught me since He said, "I am going to shake this nation." The next five chapters are a description of where we are and where we need to be. Then, the last ten chapters present the Ten Commandments of Ministry as a new code of conduct for American pastors, leaders, and believers.

We each have a unique calling in the body of Christ. We each exert influence in our families, churches, and communities. Our lives *are* our ministries, and as such, they must reflect only the highest standards of integrity. Working together, we *can* preclude the judgment of God. We *can* reestablish a committed, accountable force of spiritual Nazirites in America. We *can* turn our nation around for the next generation to finish the job.

As the Lord said to me, "I want to start with you." Let your own heart be shaken to the core. Reorganize your family, your ministry, and your future based upon these principles. Let's restore our nation—*one pastor, one leader, and one Christian at a time.*

PART 1

HELP FOR THE DYSFUNCTIONAL CHURCH

Chapter 1

Mentoring for the Unfathered Church

> For if you were to have countless tutors in Christ,
> yet you would not have many fathers, for in Christ
> Jesus I became your father through the gospel.
> Therefore I exhort you, be imitators of me. For
> this reason I have sent to you Timothy, who is my
> beloved and faithful child in the Lord, and he will
> remind you of my ways which are in Christ, just
> as I teach everywhere in every church.
>
> —1 Corinthians 4:15–17

DYSFUNCTIONAL MAY BE DEFINED AS "DEVIATING from normal behavior." In his book *The Five Dysfunctions of a Team*, Patrick Lencioni analyzes five reasons teams fail. But why do *pastors* fail? Surely there must be basic underpinnings in their foundation that support the weight of ministry for a season but eventually crack. Can we solidify a pastor emotionally and spiritually to be able to more accurately predict a lifetime of success and glory to God?

I have isolated what I believe to be the five primary dysfunctions in the American church. The cure for these dysfunctions is found in a return to the fivefold ministry pattern found in Ephesians 4:11–12: "And He gave some as apostles, and some as prophets, and some as evangelists, and some as pastors and teachers, for the equipping of the saints for the work of service, to the building up of the body of Christ."

Without the solidifying strength of these five offices, pastors are building on sand and will not survive the flood of filth, temptation, confusion, and discouragement from the enemy. To return to the fivefold ministry is not simply to welcome representatives of these five offices to preach in our pulpits, but also to establish these characteristics in our ministries. It is to have them so integral a part of our churches that pastors and believers alike embrace them as the bedrock of order and stability that they were meant to be.

If you are a pastor reading this book, you can give direction to the members and attendees of your congregation to encourage, train, and release them into ministry as teachers, prophets, or evangelists in their homes, communities, and cities. The fivefold ministry is strengthened as each Christian does his or her part in God's plan. If you are a concerned Christian who wants to do something to help bring an end to the alarming failures among pastors and Christians alike, you can diligently seek God's direction and follow the instructions He gives you—directly or through the pastor He has placed over you. Remember, you and Christians everywhere are the church—it is not a stone and glass building with no heart!

DYSFUNCTION 1: THE UNFATHERED CHURCH

It seems to me that the *primary* reason for ministerial instability and failure, and the first dysfunction in many churches, is a lack of fathering. Mentoring, or fathering, is a basic human need, and no Christian is exempt from it. Jesus Himself needed the affirming word from heaven: "You are my Son, whom I love; with you I am well pleased" (Mark 1:11, NIV). But, unfortunately, many Christians, even those in wonderful denominational structures and hierarchies, experience a general lack of affirmation and mentoring. Affirmation, however, is not optional, but totally necessary, for any person to function correctly.

I have met hundreds of American church leaders and church members who suffer from a *father wound*. Until recently that term was new to me, but it is the heart of the issue affecting the deepest recesses in the souls of men. Although women suffer too from issues with their fathers, for our purposes here, I am referring to the wound that is inflicted when a boy does not sense affirmation because of an absent, anonymous, or abusive father.

A father is *absent* if he puts his work first and fails to be there to affirm a boy's achievements. (This is the situation with many pastors' children, incidentally.) He is *anonymous* if he seems unconcerned and passive about any stages, challenges, or conquests in his son's life. Some fathers are even physically, verbally, or sexually *abusive*. The resulting father wounds they inflict gradually shape their sons' actions and reactions more than any other force.

John Eldredge, in his powerful best seller *Wild at Heart*, points out that the father wound produces *posers*: men who wrestle with the question of whether they have what it takes to be a man. When a man lacks his father's affirmation, he becomes either passive (fearful of new challenges) or aggressive (focused on affirmation by achievement).[1]

Jacob, in the Old Testament, was a poser. His brother, Esau, was his father's favorite because of his masculine prowess at hunting. Jacob, on the other hand, hung around the tents, undoubtedly trying to gain his affirmation from his mother (Gen. 25: 27). Over the years, Jacob developed a sense of rejection from his father: "Isaac...loved Esau, but Rebekah loved Jacob" (Gen. 25:28, NIV).

Eldredge correctly points out that a woman cannot truly affirm a man. She can encourage him, but she cannot answer the question of his manhood that he holds within his soul.[2] When Jacob's mother overheard that Esau was about to receive the blessing, she conspired with Jacob to imitate his brother and deceive his father. The fake clothing, the skins on his arms, and the voice change represent a man who is desperate to get his father's blessing by posing as someone else.

This need for fatherly affirmation and approval is universal. It is no respecter of persons. Whether we are pastors or laypeople, the need is so deep that, when unmet, its repercussions reverberate for years down the road. I saw this quite clearly in the life of a man with whom I am good friends. This bear of a man was for years an NFL football player. His huge six-foot-six-inch frame and deep voice, however, hid a very wounded soul. For his entire athletic career, this man had tried to get his dad to attend one of his games. In high school, college, and pro contests, he left tickets for his dad at the gate, but they were never picked up.

Finally, his dad attended a Houston Oilers' professional

game, where my friend was starting on defense. His father's presence so inspired him that he sacked the quarterback, had five unassisted tackles, and blocked a field goal. After the game, he went straight to the stands to hear his father's affirmation. The much-sought coveted blessing, however, rang out as a devastating blow: "Why did you let that little guy run right around you?" his father asked.

From that moment forward, this young man's life spun out of control. This is the same sad testimony of many men who can trace their rejection to a single moment when time stood still before their father's belittling.

A minister I know told me how time stood still for him as a ten-year-old boy when his father left home. Desperate to try to keep his dad from leaving, he put a note on the steering wheel of his father's car that read, "If you love me, please don't leave." His father simply took the note, crumpled it up, and threw it at his little boy, hitting him in the chest. The resulting rift was deep and lasted for many years. Eventually, with God's grace, the father and son repaired the relationship, and the father even attended his son's five-thousand-member church. But think of the heartache and struggle that marked both father and son for years.

I recently led a pastors' Encounter Retreat (a special type of retreat that we do at my church, Bethany World Prayer Center in Baton Rouge, Louisiana) for a large group of pastors in the Midwest. After I taught on the subject of Jacob's rejection and the father wound, a senior pastor who had built a beautiful new sanctuary for his one-thousand-member congregation approached me and said, "I am Jacob."

At three months of age, this man had lost his father and had searched unsuccessfully for a spiritual mentor to affirm him as well as hold him accountable. He told me he felt insecure and unstable for no obvious reason. He and his beautiful wife had prayed concerning his unfounded anxiety that he might fall into sin and somehow destroy his precious young children.

After prayer that morning, God healed his heart, and the following day, he proactively moved toward formalizing a father relationship with senior ministry in his life. What if thousands of wounded pastors whose identities are wrapped up in achievement could find the mentoring stability of spiritual fathers who notice and affirm them? What would happen if church members who are walking around with gaping holes in their hearts could find the balm of fatherly affirmation they so desperately crave? The entire face of American Christianity, I believe, would change.

I have to give honor to my own father in this regard. His more than sixty years of marriage and ministry without blemish have built a deep foundation of stability in my life. As a young basketball player, I remember when the gym door opened and that certain medium-height man climbed the bleachers to sit on the top row. My back straightened, my gait quickened, and I played with total focus. His one sentence of affirmation, both in those games and later in my years of accomplishment, has been the lifeline of my success.

But what about the tens of thousands of Christians who lack that inward strength that comes only from affirmation? In a pastors' retreat that we did together, James Robison told what it was like when his single-parent mother gave him up to a pastor who fostered him until he was ten. When his mother came back for him, he remembers being dragged from under his bed, with his fingernails scraping across the floor. He struggled with validation his entire ministry life, and it eventually brought him to the brink of flirting with temptation in the moral area.

In the mid-1990s, however, he was set free and has since established himself as one of the most compassionate leaders to the hurting and destitute. His testimony gives hope to all that God can heal their hearts and establish them as real, functional, transparent believers, even though they may not have had the benefit of a natural father or an affirming one.

THE CURE: GOVERNMENT AND
MENTORING THROUGH THE APOSTLE

All church government should flow from an environment of affirmation, validation, and acceptance. Whether in a denomination or in a nonaligned church, pastors and church members need spiritual fathers. The early church did not develop a bureaucratic, hands-off oversight that only inspected properties and counted nickels and noses. They had overseers and elders who provided a mentoring structure to affirm, advise, and correct, if necessary.

Government is the operation of seasoned spiritual fathers who develop and mentor protégés as though they were sons. Should a default of some type occur in a church with proper government, the senior pastor clearly knows who is in charge to restore or replace him. Additionally, the members are secure because they know that not anything goes and that even a much-loved pastor who violates the predetermined boundaries will be removed and prevented from harming the sheep.

Government provides the apostolic function in ministry. This need for oversight is more adequately filled in denominational circles; in tens of thousands of independent American churches, however, it is woefully absent. But even good denominational leaders strong on government are realizing the importance of balancing that aspect with fatherly affirmation. As a result, entire denominations are transitioning to a style of oversight that is not bureaucratic and official, but that includes fathering and mentoring. Without this shift, the "wheels" of the "vehicle" are apt to fall off. Without spiritual fathers, even successful church leaders too often crash and burn because of their inward insecurities.

A secondary function of spiritual fathers is to be sure that the sons come together. In Baton Rouge, we have had a successful monthly meeting of twelve to fifteen area pastors for five years now. We call ourselves the Progressive Pastors and together represent most of the larger churches in our city. Although we hail from various groups and denominations, we all crave fellowship, fathering, and affirmation.

Before we came together, the walls of insecurity and competition among us were rather high. When we began meeting, we committed to rotate to a different church each month and not to miss a meeting unless we were out of town. Now, with almost 100 percent attendance each month, the pastors in this group have regularly preached at one another's churches, and there is no sense of posing, impressing, or competing. We stand together, work together, laugh together, and minister to one another. This is the by-product of a fathering, mentoring, and accountable sense of government in a city.

Every Christian needs something similar in his own life, and in my opinion, a small group where mentoring and fathering takes place is what works best. Here at Bethany, we have scores of men's (and women's) small groups that meet weekly, where seasoned leaders work with younger men. In a fatherless generation, we have found that men respond best in a mentoring type of relationship to a man about ten years older (or more) than they. Even hard-core recovering drug users, persons with criminal records, and young men from fatherless homes are responding incredibly to the affirmation of a Christian mentor who tracks their progress and expresses his joy and pride in their accomplishment. Such is the effect of real, transparent, life-affirming relationships between men in the body of Christ.

As I write this chapter, I am speaking at a large ministers' fellowship of nonaligned, independent churches in the Northwest. Over seven hundred pastors call this group "home," and it is led by a seasoned seventy-seven-year-old spiritual father. His gentle, soft-spoken manner belies the fact that hundreds of pastors and major apostolic figures from around the world happily relate to him.

From India, Brazil, and Europe, they are here because of his calm affirmation and steady forward vision to missions. Their deep admiration for his forty years of successful pastoring and his lack of pressure, control, and agenda make them long for and welcome his mentoring in their lives. This gentle man has empowered eleven regional directors in the United States, who work in the same spirit with those geographically nearby.

Let's follow this godly man's example and turn this ship around! It's time for pastors to find their spiritual mentors, the ones they look to for affirmation and validation. It's time for them to tell their congregations who those people are and set up regular interaction with them. It's time for Christians everywhere to recognize the importance of spiritual fathering and to begin finding ways to give and receive the fathering they so desperately need.

With this multitude of counsel, all Christians can have a source of help for making major decisions and seeking direction. Then, when they have found their spiritual fathers, they can in turn look for peers, perhaps a little younger than they, who desperately crave affirmation. Thus a chain of empowerment and accountability will be set up, all flowing from the apostolic anointing of Jesus and His relationship to His Father: "That they may all be one; even as You, Father, are in Me and I in You, that they also may be in Us, so that the world may believe that You sent Me" (John 17:21).

The apostolic gift brings affirmation and corrects the first dysfunction in the church, but there is a second much-needed dimension for spiritual leaders: the prophetic. This office of the fivefold ministry brings confrontation, accountability, and discipline and is the second issue addressed when dealing with church dysfunction.

QUESTIONS TO THINK ABOUT

1. What shift have you seen in the American family that has led to this present fatherless generation? Have you experienced the absence of a strong, nurturing father influence in your life? How did it affect you?

2. How do Christians who have suffered father wounds sometimes carry this over into their relationships in the body of Christ?

3. Believers often assume that their pastors have it all together and don't suffer the same wounds or go through the same struggles as ordinary Christians. Why is this not true, and how does it harm pastors when their members think like this?

4. Have you had the benefit of an older, more mature Christian taking you under his or her wing? If so, how did it help shape your Christian walk? If not, are you open to this type of relationship? Why or why not?

5. Have you ever had the privilege of being someone's mentor? If so, what particular challenges did you face? What rewards did you receive from the relationship? If you have never mentored someone, would you be willing for God to use you in this way? Why or why not?

CHAPTER 2

STANDARDS FOR THE UNCORRECTED CHURCH

Do not receive an accusation against an elder except on the basis of two or three witnesses. Those who continue in sin, rebuke in the presence of all, so that the rest also will be fearful of sinning. I solemnly charge you in the presence of God and of Christ Jesus and of His chosen angels, to maintain these principles without bias, doing nothing in a spirit of partiality.

—1 TIMOTHY 5:19–21

IN BOTH THE OLD AND NEW TESTAMENTS, THE prophet was an individual who ministered from a position of objectivity. He "called it like it was" and dared to confront king and clergy alike. Nathan confronted David, Elijah confronted Ahab, and John confronted Herod. Accountability was built into the prophetic office and was intended to bring deliverance rather than destruction.

David was a good king but not a very good father. His son Adonijah was very strong-willed, and David "never disciplined him at any time, even by asking, 'What are you doing?'" (1 Kings 1:6, NLT). As a result, Adonijah became a rebellious plague to the nation. What did David, the father, think would happen if he allowed his strong-willed son to grow in influence without facing consequences for his undesirable behavior?

In their best-selling book *Boundaries with Kids*, Dr. Henry Cloud and Dr. John Townsend provide a formula for raising a functional child: freedom equals choices, which equals consequences, which equals love.[1] God gave Adam and Eve freedom to eat from any tree in the garden, with one exception. Their wrong choice led to a previously determined consequence: "You shall surely die" (Gen. 2:17, NKJV). Their wrong choice also brought expulsion from Eden, just as God had said it would. But that expulsion, though a justifiable consequence, came with and demonstrated God's love. He showed mercy to them by covering them with skins, but in no way did He change the consequences of their actions.

Drs. Cloud and Townsend point out that we often interrupt the natural law of sowing and reaping when dealing with our children. However, there can be no character change without pain. A child who never feels the pain of wrong choices will repeat them every time.[2]

It is the same with spiritual leaders and all who follow Christ. Why should we think that those who experience no consequences for their poor choices will change or do anything differently? Paul said, "No discipline seems pleasant at the time, but painful. Later on, however, it produces a harvest of righteousness and peace for those who have been trained by it" (Heb. 12:11, NIV).

When you allow the consequences that result from poor

financial choices, people learn not to overspend. When you allow a child to go to jail and refuse to bail him or her out for driving one hundred miles an hour or doing drugs, that child learns to value a driver's license or a safe environment. Our culture of entitlement, unfortunately, has produced a spoiled generation of children who repeatedly have to be asked, "What do you say?" after receiving an expensive Christmas present!

DYSFUNCTION 2: THE UNCORRECTED CHURCH

It is much the same in the dysfunctional church. Not only is it unfathered, but it is also uncorrected. When Christian leaders commit moral failure but opt out of their supposed spiritual oversight, *there was none to begin with.* These leaders may have pretended to be submitted and accountable, but unless accountability is legally a part of their churches' bylaws, it is easy to circumvent. When Christian believers change churches as though they were simply changing clothes, could it be that deep inside they don't want to be accountable to anyone and cover it by saying they feel "led" to go elsewhere?

One of America's top Christian leaders lamented to me about the number of high-profile ministers who considered him their spiritual accountability but did not communicate with him for years at a time. When their moral failures surfaced, those familiar with the "relationships" questioned his lack of action. As we were discussing this, I told him, "Without it being written into bylaws, you have no authority to act." He answered, "I wish you would write a book on that." So that's what I'm doing.

The story of a particular megachurch pastor, who was in close relationship to his founding overseer for almost twenty years, amazed me. As the overseer visited the pastor every month to encourage him and help him build, the church grew from a handful of people to more than four thousand. But then an accusation against the pastor of an inappropriate relationship surfaced. The overseer confronted the pastor, but to no avail. The pastor ended the relationship with the overseer and continued in his devastating direction, right before the eyes of the watching community and to the great detriment of the congregation.

As goes the pastor, so goes the congregation. When the pastor is a lone ranger who answers to no one but the Lord, is it any wonder that his people adopt the same stance? When a loving leader tries to talk to them about a moral failing or when the pastor begins challenging their comfort zone and exhorting them to live out their faith, they quietly (and sometimes not so quietly) pack their bags and leave. After all, this is America, and nobody has the right to tell us what to do, right?

Wrong! Every one of us must be accountable to others for what we do or don't do. We bear the responsibility for our decisions, and when we violate the standards of God's Word, we should expect to suffer the consequences. But vague expectations and choices without consequences bring confusion. Even the world knows this. Politicians face serious consequences with their constituents when they commit moral failure. Athletes who break the rules, throw temper tantrums, or use drugs are often required to sit out entire seasons. Can the church require less of its own?

The world looks upon the church's abuse of authority and lack of accountability as the ultimate hypocrisy. The body of Christ and its leaders must have spiritual fathers in their lives who act both in the role of affirmation (the apostle) and the role of correction (the prophet). After all, God deals in grace and truth (John 1:17).

THE CURE: ACCOUNTABILITY AND STANDARDS THROUGH THE PROPHET

Paul taught in 1 Timothy 5:21 that we should "maintain these principles without bias, doing nothing in the spirit of partiality." If you become so spiritually puffed up that you no longer feel anyone can correct and discipline you, you have exempted yourself from the discipline of principle and require that *your* discipline be relational. When consequences are relational and not reality-based (pain), no character change occurs.

Drs. Cloud and Townsend point out that relational consequences such as nagging, guilt, and withholding affection never really change character. Only reality-based consequences (automatic consequences that result directly from actions and choices) change us. Although we may try to manipulate and maneuver our way out of the problems we have caused, the consequences still must happen if we are to learn, grow, and change.[3]

"What about compassion and empathy?" you might wonder. God empathized with Adam and Eve by covering their sin with skins. He forgave them and continued to love them, but He allowed their consequences to fall upon them. How confused are parents and church leaders who fail to deliver promised consequences, thus preventing them from having a chance to do their work in an individual!

"A man of great anger will bear the penalty, for if you *rescue* him, you will only have to do it again" (Prov. 19:19, emphasis added). Allowing consequences to occur sends a message to the soul of the one involved: *I can't maneuver my way out.* We may love, support, empathize, assist, and encourage—but never rescue.

This is the principle of *standards* in action. A thirteen-inch, one-foot ruler is ridiculous. In fact, it is impossible, because the standard for a ruler is twelve inches and twelve inches only. In similar fashion, the role of the prophet is to remind us of and to enforce God's standards.

Can the church be self-governing? Does it have the guts to stand up and correct itself? Do leaders and believers possess the courage to arrange for their own discipline and allow the process to work, even when they disagree? Will they submit to the prophetic oversight of seasoned men who lovingly recommend a course of action that is honorable, even when others protest they don't "feel the love"? If the American church will commit to higher ethical and moral standards than even the medical or legal professions endure, the world will once again look to us for moral direction.

Fathering for an unfathered church and standards for an uncorrected church will lay a new foundation for touching America. Security and sincerity will reign. I believe Americans will run by the millions to be part of something relational and real. The cross will be restored to rightful prominence. Evangelism will become natural as the church becomes irresistible to the lost. The lost art of discipleship will return to congregations, and millions of unfruitful believers will enter into what we have always dreamed of: multiplication.

QUESTIONS TO THINK ABOUT

1. This chapter presents the equation, "Freedom equals choices, which equals consequences, which equals love." How is it actually a demonstration of love to allow people to face the consequences for their actions? How does it demonstrate lack of love to rescue people from the consequences of their chosen behavior?

2. Have you ever had to let a loved one suffer consequences for an action while everything in you wanted to alleviate the pain? What gave you the strength to do the right thing, and what long-term results occurred in the life of your loved one?

3. If God forgives us for our sins, why do we still, most of the time, have to suffer the consequences? Have you ever experienced this? What did you learn from it?

4. Why is it not enough for a pastor to say he answers to God and therefore does not need to be accountable to anyone else? Why do some believers accept this excuse?

5. In your opinion, do pastors and believers answer to different standards before God? Why or why not?

CHAPTER 3

MULTIPLICATION FOR THE UNFRUITFUL CHURCH

I chose you, and appointed you that you would go
and bear fruit, and that your fruit would remain.
—JOHN 15:16

JESUS PASSED A FIG TREE AND REBUKED IT FOR HAVING nothing but leaves. It is possible to have *results* without having *fruit*. Fruit remains: "I chose you, and appointed you that you would go and bear fruit, and that your fruit would remain" (John 15:16). That is Jesus's mandate to us, but sadly, too few are actually fulfilling that command and producing fruit that remains.

DYSFUNCTION 3: UNFRUITFULNESS

Unfruitfulness is the third dysfunction in the American church, and it relates to the office of the evangelist. But the problem comes because our typical idea of evangelism centers upon an event, a crusade, or a program. Through these venues, we may see scores of responses, but five years later there is no lasting fruit.

"If these events are so unfruitful," you might wonder, "who, then, is filling our churches to record crowds?" The answer is that much of our perceived growth is simply transfer growth, the movement of believers from church to church. Someone said that transfer growth is similar to getting everyone in a room to change chairs within the room. There's a great deal of activity and bustle, but nothing really changes.

When the same thing happens in our churches, the net result for the kingdom of God is zero. Our best weekend efforts at captivating or entertaining crowds may be accomplishing *addition* to our particular church, but that is not *multiplication*. It is not producing fruit that remains.

There are basically three levels of participation in every church: *attenders*, *members*, and *multipliers*. Attenders are those who sporadically make a certain church their head-quarters. They make no commitment in finances, attendance, or small-group involvement, but they consider a particular church "their church," especially at Christmas and Easter.

I once encountered this "attender" mind-set in a man I ran into at a local gas station. As is often my custom, I asked, "What church do you attend?" When he answered that he attended Bethany (my church), I decided to delve a little deeper. "Don't they have three campuses? Which do you attend?" I casually questioned. The man proudly announced that he attended our north campus, and I responded with, "Really? Who's the pastor of the church?" Well, the man couldn't answer, and I'm sure you can imagine the look on his face when I calmly replied, "I'm the pastor."

That, my friend, is an attender!

Members go to a second, higher level of involvement, with

commitment to weekly attendance, tithing, and small-group participation. Members are progressing toward discipleship but may not necessarily walk in purity, carry a burden for the lost, or know how to disciple someone else. This is where true evangelism comes into play.

True evangelism springs from discipleship. Believers come alive when someone removes the dead branches of sin, bondage, and fear from their lives. When they are intentionally discipled, they are empowered to break through the *member* ceiling and move up to the level of a *multiplier*. This responsibility of discipling is a task reserved for not only the pastor but also for everyone who calls himself a follower of Christ. We all must be discipling others, who in turn disciple others.

THE CURE: MULTIPLICATION THROUGH THE EVANGELIST

Growing mature believers is what guarantees multiplication, and the discipleship that makes it happen is seen in the office of the evangelist. Paul described this phenomenon in 2 Timothy 2:2: "The things which you have heard from me in the presence of many witnesses, entrust these to faithful men who will be able to teach others also." The early church had no buildings, props, or sound systems. What they did have was one-on-one discipleship, and that system released an organic power that filled the entire known world.

Let's look at Paul's method of growing the church by growing its members: "Him we preach, warning every man and teaching every man in all wisdom, that we may present every man perfect in Christ Jesus" (Col. 1:28, NKJV).

1. "Him we preach" (winning souls)

It all starts here when we proclaim the gospel and a sinner responds. However, most of us stop here and call it evangelism. This, however, is addition; every step after this is what brings multiplication.

2. "Warning every man" (sanctifying the body, mind, and spirit)

This includes the intentional breaking of habits, bondages, and strongholds in the lives of new believers. The focus is on getting them free from the negative influences that destroy. At Bethany we use our Journey classes and Encounter Retreat weekends to accomplish this (twelve weeks of classes, including the weekend retreat).

3. "Teaching every man" (imparting wisdom and order through the Scriptures)

This refers to line-upon-line doctrinal and biblical studies to build faith, purpose, vision, and serious discipleship. At Bethany we do this in three twelve-week terms of instruction in family, finances, relationships, prayer, doctrine, and ministry training. We call these classes the Discovery.

4. "Present every man perfect in Christ Jesus" (multiplication)

Now we are ready to multiply! God can take "template" Christians and stamp them across the lives of other new believers. A truly discipled believer is God's greatest evangelistic tool.

Dr. Bill Bright, founder of Campus Crusade for Christ, illustrated these strategies in his book *5 Steps to Making Disciples.* He gave the example of one of his disciples who went back to Thailand and discipled seven hundred believers. One of those seven hundred preached personally to over two hundred thousand people in his lifetime and saw more than twenty thousand receive Christ![1] That is multiplication—not an event or fruitless effort at entertainment, but a chain reaction of changed lives that exponentially grows.

Bethany now does missions with a multiplication model in place. In the year 2000, I was speaking to a representative of the Gideons International, the Bible distribution organization that delivers millions of copies of the Bible annually. He explained that they had divided the world into twelve regions, and he was over the Middle Eastern area. I sensed an impression from the Lord in that conversation that I was to do missions in that way for at least the next decade.

I started with the Gideons' map of the world zones and found in each zone a solid missions leader with whom I was already working. In 2001, we all met in Zurich, Switzerland, and laid out a strategy for each man to find and groom the best national leader he could locate in each of the fifteen to twenty nations in his zone. Two years later, as that task began to be complete, we commissioned all of those national leaders to find a team of leaders (up to twelve) in their own countries.

We committed financially to fund for one year any good national pastor who would plant a church and be accountable in his ministry to one of our network leaders. We began to plant churches in various denominations all across the world, and the Global 12 Project was born.

That simple network has now planted over sixteen thousand churches as of January 2008. Our studies show that for every church we as westerners paid for, the national leaders have paid for four more. Multiplication is occurring because of a multiplication of accountable leaders. The results have been amazing, and we have had single donations of up to one million dollars given to plant almost nine hundred churches at a time!

What would happen in America if we had churches full of multipliers? What would happen if they would each win a soul and then get that person delivered of inner bondages and wounds and fully trained to set others free? Each person discipled would set off a chain reaction of multiplication, and the church would no longer depend on the personality or presence of a charismatic pastor but on thousands of "ambassadors."

This is what the early church did without benefit of buildings, Bibles, tapes, CDs, books, concerts, dramas, computers, television, or radio. Their focus was on making disciples and multiplying them. When we get our thinking straight about what is a normal, functional church, the pressure of performance will cease.

As I write this chapter, I am on my way to Korea to speak in the world's largest church, Yoido Full Gospel Church, in Seoul, South Korea. With seven hundred fifty thousand members, their history records times when they had as many as fifty thousand active cell groups. Dr. David Yonggi Cho, the pastor, would "allow" the groups to evangelize only one family every six months, and they still added fifty thousand new members! This explosive evangelism happened in the hands of the ordinary, rank-and-file believers—not from some big-name personality summoned to draw a crowd.

Yoido Full Gospel is team ministry at its best. True discipleship is thriving as a result of the huge net of connected relationships drawn weekly across the length and breadth of Seoul's hurting masses. Churches worldwide have replicated, modified, and adapted Dr. Cho's model to become powerful centers of discipleship and multiplication. The untapped power of the average believer has been unleashed, and real growth in God's kingdom is occurring as one-on-one discipleship has come to the forefront of personal and corporate ministry.

Fathering comes from the *apostolic* mentoring, affirmation, and government so needed for today's Christians. *Correction* comes from fearless *prophetic* accountability willing to maintain standards, enforce consequences of failure, and extend merciful empathy in changing the character of fallen leaders and believers. *Fruitfulness* comes from *evangelism* coupled with intentional discipleship, and the result is multiplication.

The healing of the dysfunctional church would not be complete, however, without pastors. "He gave some pastors" to heal the inner wounds and struggles of believers. Pastors are the second phase in Paul's Colossians 1:28 model: "warning every man."

QUESTIONS TO THINK ABOUT

1. What is the difference between attenders, members, and multipliers in a church? Which level are you in? Which level would you like to be in? What steps will you take to get there?

2. Why does simply getting people saved never result in multiplication in the church? What is the missing ingredient to seeing explosive multiplication? Why do most Christians overlook this basic fact?

3. In this chapter, the following statement is made: "A truly discipled believer is God's greatest evangelistic tool." Do you agree with this statement? Why or why not?

4. What are we the church responsible for after leading people to Christ? What are the best ways of accomplishing these goals? How can each member of the church play a vital role in discipling new believers?

5. Have you personally ever led someone to Christ? If so, what was that experience like, both for you and the person you led to the Lord? If not, what is the single greatest barrier keeping you from becoming a soulwinner?

CHAPTER 4

HEALING FOR THE UNHEALED CHURCH

They have healed the brokenness of My people superficially, saying, "Peace, peace," but there is no peace.

—JEREMIAH 6:14

THE FOURTH DYSFUNCTION OF THE AMERICAN church is that it is wounded and unhealed. Jeremiah recognized this and spoke of it in Jeremiah 6:14. The New King James Version expresses it this way: "They have also healed the hurt of my people slightly, saying 'Peace, peace!' when there is no peace"; and the New Century Version says, "They tried to heal my people's serious injuries as if they were small wounds. They said, 'It's all right, it's all right.' But really, it is not all right."

DYSFUNCTION 4: THE UNHEALED CHURCH

An unhealed church has deep inner wounds that only the cross can heal. As the message of the cross moves further from the center of attention, we polarize around personalities

(1 Cor. 1). The cross, however, is the central message of the church because it destroys pride, frees from bondage, releases blessing, and brings people together.

At Bethany we have seen over ten thousand of our members attend our Encounter Retreat weekends. In eight powerful sessions, believers visit the cross to deal with rejection (father wounds), unforgiveness, spiritual and mental ties with demonic strongholds (often acquired ignorantly), and sexual bondage. How can we think that new believers can fill out a card or pray a sinner's prayer but have no need to deal with emotional and mental scars that took a lifetime to create?

The power of the cross to change lives is evidenced in one of our strongest leaders at Bethany. This man now has his own incredibly successful insurance company and productive Christian life, but that wasn't always the case. You would never know by looking at him that this man had once been a drug user, gambler, and womanizer (even though he had attended a Christian university!). Although he possessed immense personal giftings, they were completely overshadowed by his driven appetites.

Invited to attend an Encounter Retreat, the man agreed to go, and there on that momentous weekend, he was delivered from cocaine addiction and a host of other vices. He and his beautiful wife are now front-row Bethany believers, his business is prospering, and he leads a small group for men recovering from drugs. He even teaches sometimes at our Encounter Retreats, and his real-life testimony to the power of the cross to totally transform hearts makes him a favorite each time.

In many of our churches, however, the cross is considered excess baggage, the holdover message from the last century that does not relate to the iPhone generation. We hide it, disguise it, and move past it. We motivate, entertain, and impress as our key members continue to divorce, look at pornography, and raise rebellious, wild children. That is what happens when we forget the cross and its powerful message and deny its power to those who so desperately need it.

The cross was the secret to Israel's healing in the wilderness. Their murmuring and complaining allowed a plague of demonic snakes into the camp. Only a revelation of the cross in the wilderness neutralized that poison (Num. 21:8). In the same way, the poison from our past can be supernaturally removed by a glimpse backward to the events of the cross.

What does it do in the hearts of believers when they get a revelation of the cross? It is no less life-saving than it was for Israel in the wilderness. By studying the wounds of Christ, believers can receive faith for deliverance in every area. Listed below are some of the things that believers need to know are theirs because of what Christ suffered in His body:

1. Peace (His brow)

Christ began to taste the cup of anxiety, tribulation, and pressure in Gethsemane. He chose the will of God and paid the highest price. The blood came to the surface of His skin and ruptured capillaries, a phenomenon resulting from extreme mental pressure. *Jesus took my cares, worries, and anxieties upon Himself and gave me peace.*

2. Healing (His back)

Isaiah and Peter both prophesied, "By His wounds you were healed" (1 Pet. 2:24). One of the duties of the Roman lictor was to scourge criminals. Using a whip with razor-sharp

tentacles embedded with lead and bone, the lictor system-
atically shredded the victim's back as he inflicted the brutal
scourging. As the beating occurred, the tortuous tentacles
of the whip flew wildly across the victim's back and wrapped
around to his front, often horribly disfiguring him. No wonder
Isaiah said, "His appearance was so disfigured beyond that of
any man and his form marred beyond human likeness" (Isa.
52:14, NIV). *Jesus bore my pain and agony so I could be healed
in every dimension of life.*

3. Forgiveness (His hands)

Colossians 2:14 says that He, "having canceled out the
certificate of debt consisting of decrees against us, which was
hostile to us…has taken it out of the way, having nailed it to the
cross." A certificate of debt (IOU), in Jesus's day, was a hand-
written promissory note. The ancient method of debt cancella-
tion involved driving a nail through the note and posting it on
the purchased property when the debt was paid.

Every sin in our past is a legal IOU in our own hand-
writing. When Christ was crucified, our list of spiritual IOUs
was nailed between His hands and the cross. *The debt, the
promissory note, the arrest warrant are all marked "Canceled"
when I receive Jesus's forgiveness.*

4. Victory (His feet)

Colossians continues, "And having disarmed the powers
and authorities, he made a public spectacle of them, triumphing
over them by the cross" (v. 15, NIV). After a Roman military
triumph, the victor always placed his foot upon the neck of the
prostrate fallen general, much as Joshua did to the five kings at
Makkedah (Josh. 10:16). Christians should look at every difficult

circumstance from the perspective of the victory of the cross and resurrection. *By His death on the cross, Jesus put my weakness, fear, and defeat under His feet* (Eph. 1:22).

5. Blessing (His head)

The thorn is first mentioned in Genesis 3:18 as part of the curse that came upon Adam. Christ was crowned with thorns, symbolizing His taking of the pain, suffering, and poverty that entered the world after Adam and Eve's sin. The crown of thorns Jesus wore represents the crushing of the spirit of poverty, debt, and lack. *Because of that, I can know that "my God will supply all [my] needs according to His riches in glory in Christ Jesus"* (Phil. 4:19).

6. Inner healing (His side)

The piercing of Christ's side represents the breaking of the heart. *The inner wounds and heartbreak of my experiences and circumstances are healed as I release bitterness and experience forgiveness.*

THE CURE: HEALING THROUGH THE PASTOR

The healing and deliverance of believers is truly the work of the pastor, the fourth listing in the fivefold ministry callings. A pastor sees his members not as numbers, but as gifted, talented leaders whose potential must be released. David said, "Heal my soul" (Ps. 41:4). He obviously understood the pastoral process because he took about four hundred men who were in debt, in distress, and in discontent (1 Sam. 22:2) and from them formed the mightiest warriors in history.

In the same way, the thousands packing our churches must

have individual attention and healing. I once met with the staff of a twenty-five-thousand-member church and was shocked to find fewer than five pastors relying merely on a counseling and benevolence office to meet the needs of the flock. This pulpit-driven megachurch was not even attempting to meet the true inner needs of its members by giving individual attention to its disciples.

One reason too few believers are finding the help they need is that the pastors themselves need healing. "Physician, heal yourself" (Luke 4:23) was a popular proverb in Jesus's day to express how often the "doctor" himself is sick. To counter that tendency in the church, some other men of God and I are now conducting pastors' Encounter Retreats in major cities across America in order to give pastors a safe place to release the bitterness, rejection, frustration, and temptation they deal with as shepherds. These powerful retreats are much like the Encounter Retreats we hold for individual believers at Bethany, but in a protected, emotionally safe environment for ministry leaders. Once the pastors are healed, they can go home and become conduits of healing for their congregations.

Regardless of the format or methods we use to bring healing (and there are many), the bottom line is that most Christians have only come out of "Egypt" but not yet entered the "promised land" of happy marriages, stable emotions, and holy lives. In the story of the good Samaritan, the good Samaritan not only resuscitated the stranger but also "bandaged up his wounds, pouring oil and wine on them...and brought him to an inn and took care of him" (Luke 10:34). The professional clergy of the day neither noticed nor helped the poor stranger, but the good Samaritan did what the professionals did not and ministered to every area of need.

This highlights a second reason the church is unpastored: too many pastors are trying to do it all themselves. They hold the reins of ministry and either don't realize or downright refuse to empower the flock to participate in the high calling of pastoring. But when they see that pastoring, like discipleship, is really the responsibility of all the body of Christ, they will bring mature believers alongside them in the ministry and release them into their own good Samaritan–type acts of love and service.

I remember my first attempt at scuba diving, off the coast of Australia at the Great Barrier Reef. Below the surface were the strangest creatures imaginable: four-foot tall clams with neon-blue mouths, strange fish, and a host of exaggerated marine bodies I had never seen. When I surfaced, however, there were the yachts with the bikini-clad sunbathers: the "nice people." Below was the "underworld," full of many strange creatures; above was the "overworld," full of those who seemingly had it all together.

We Christians tend to focus on the overworld, the straight, two-car, suburban, tax-paying, tithing yuppie family. We tend to distance ourselves from those who are too different, too odd, too disturbing to our genteel sensibilities. Jesus, however, took the underworld—the outcasts, the tax collectors, the demonized, and the poor—and pastored them. He turned them into apostles, prophets, deacons, and leaders. We can do no less.

The good Samaritan represents a paradigm shift in our number-crunching, parking-lot counting, budget-setting, and buildings mentality. The nameless victim he discovered on the side of the road demanded his full attention, and he gave it. He, in effect, became a *pastor of one*, and that is the challenge for every single Christian in every single church. Maybe we cannot take care of everybody, but each one of us can take care of one other person, caring for his needs, showing him the way, and, in effect, pastoring him to wholeness and maturity.

America has become so dysfunctional that it could be characterized a post-Christian society. The bed-hopping, drug-crazed, multiple-marriage family has produced what some psychiatrists are calling flatliners: people with no feeling, people whose hearts are stone. Many youth are approaching this status; as a result, it takes more and more stimulation to even evoke compassion in them.

We need to quit peeking at the "fastest growing" list and start looking at the "best pastored" list (you won't find it). A truly well-pastored church is one in which each member's inner wounds are healed and inner gifts and talents released—a church in which no one is anonymous; couples aren't living together; and no one is bitter, addicted, and unhealed.

How do we accomplish this? More staff? There is no way, with just more staff, to enter into the depth of personal ministry needed. But when the church becomes an army of multipliers, thickening the core of ministry, each believer takes on the job of discipling "one," of becoming a pastor of one.

The Samaritan willingly devoted massive amounts of his time and money to be sure his anonymous "project" fully recovered in the inn. But in many of our churches today, follow-up is nonexistent. We report our statistics, but we forget our calling: "Now to Him who is able to keep you from stumbling, and to present you faultless before the presence of His glory with exceeding joy" (Jude 24, NKJV).

Week after week, as I stand in the lobby of my church shaking hands with our members, I look into the faces of the thousands walking by and think: "Are they healed… happy…holy? Are they conquering temptation? Are they active in their ministry? Are their children warriors of faith? Are they tithers and givers? Are their extended families saved? What inner battles are they fighting behind the smile? What insecurities haunt them? What habits are they trapped in, unable to break free from?"

But in the midst of all these questions running through my mind, I recognize people whose testimonies from their Encounter Retreat experiences attest to their change:

- ⊰⊱ A woman who would not leave her home because of a fear of everything but who is now going by herself to Wal-Mart and to church.

- ⊰⊱ A depressed, suicidal man who came to service on Wednesday night, got saved, attended the Encounter Retreat that same weekend, and is now filled with the joy of the Lord.

- ⊰⊱ A Buddhist plumber who came to Easter service, went on the Encounter Retreat, and has now been free for six months. He testified he had given up on church but is now happy and bringing his family and friends to events.

The time has come for the American church to get serious about pastoring. It is hard work to help our members put their lives in order, but, as the previous chapter showed, it has "multiple" rewards. The healed church will be the conquering church. And after we have a healed church, let's do the final thing needed to heal the dysfunctional church: let's go back to the Bible.

QUESTIONS TO THINK ABOUT

1. How do you think it is possible for a person to come to Christ and yet remain emotionally wounded and unhealed? Was this your experience? What helped you find wholeness in Christ?

2. What does it mean to have a revelation of the cross? Why is this the single most important factor to bringing spiritual and emotional healing to a person?

3. In the body of Christ, whose responsibility is it to see that people live in wholeness? Why do we sometimes act as though this is the pastor's responsibility—not ours?

4. Did someone ever reach out to you in Christian love when you really needed it and helped you find healing? What was the circumstance, and how did their love affect you? What could you do to minister this same type of love to someone else?

5. What does the phrase *pastor of one* mean? Does it describe you? Could you release your faith to believe that you could disciple one other person and lead that person into wholeness? What fears are holding you back?

CHAPTER 5

THE SCRIPTURES FOR THE UNTAUGHT CHURCH

> From childhood you have known the sacred
> writings which are able to give you the wisdom
> that leads to salvation through faith which is in
> Christ Jesus. All Scripture is inspired by God
> and profitable for teaching, for reproof, for
> correction, for training in righteousness; so that
> the man of God may be adequate, equipped for
> every good work.
>
> —2 TIMOTHY 3:15–17

DYSFUNCTION 5: THE UNTAUGHT CHURCH

The fifth dysfunction of the American church is that it is untaught. Though tapes, CDs, DVDs, television programs, and books abound, the average American Christian still remains ignorant of an intermediate knowledge of the Scripture, even after years of sitting under pastoral ministry.

My wife and I were staying at a hotel on the shore of the Sea of Galilee on our thirtieth anniversary. It was Mother's Day, and the day before we had visited the Shrine of the Book in Jerusalem. This fabulous display shows the Jewish people's commitment, as "keepers of the book," to track down worldwide every syllable of Scripture.

As I sat in the bed and drank a cup of coffee, suddenly my mother-in-law's face came before my spirit (I made no connection with the holiday). The voice of the Lord spoke inwardly to me and asked, "Have you ever known anyone who loved My Word more than My servant Pat?" Pat Clark, who has been with the Lord for eighteen years, loved the reading, singing, and teaching of the Scripture as much as anyone I have ever known. The Lord continued, "I want you to spend the rest of your life teaching My people the Scripture. Many are ignorant of My Word, and I want you to teach them."

There in the bed, I began to weep as this mandate settled in my spirit. Many American churches have become a mile wide and an inch deep when it comes to biblical knowledge. Sadly, the Scriptures are moving more and more to the bottom shelf in our priorities.

The next Sunday after we returned home, we honored all high school and college graduates in our services. Many of the high school students were graduating from our own Christian school, and I decided to take a random survey of their Bible knowledge. At the four services that weekend, I asked the more than two hundred graduates if any of them knew anything from John 13 (none did), Acts 13 (none did), and Romans 13 (none did). When I mentioned 1 Corinthians 13 (the love chapter), quite a few raised their hands.

What has happened to the line-upon-line exposition of the Scriptures? What has happened to produce an entire generation of American Christians who do not know even the most basic Bible stories and elementary doctrine?

Paul reminded Timothy that he, Timothy, had known the Holy Scriptures since childhood, as early childhood for the Hebrews always included memorizing the Torah. Many of us, unfortunately, have "progressed" past a reliance on the Scriptures and have substituted motivational relevance for Bible knowledge. Pastors preach it, and believers eagerly lap it up.

Don't get me wrong; I am definitely in favor of relevant messages because the attention deficit of this generation usually prevents them from even reading, let alone studying or intently learning, the Scriptures. However, the goal of our creative approaches to preaching should be to aid in understanding and applying the Scriptures, not in becoming self-help and motivational gurus. What is wrong with a pastor using all his powers of persuasion and clarity to help people understand, apply, and transmit the Scriptures to others? Nothing—and it's time to bring it back!

The physical body will crave that which you feed it. If high-calorie, high-fat items are on the daily menu, the body soon loses its appetite for the more nutritious whole grains, fruits, and vegetables. If believers constantly gorge on spiritual junk food of little spiritual value, they soon lose their hunger for the eternal, life-changing Word of God. So the responsibility is shared: pastors must teach the pure, unadulterated Word, and believers must relish that which is wholesome and readily accept it, even if it does not seem as trendy or exciting as the latest spiritual fad.

THE CURE: INSTRUCTION IN THE HOLY
SCRIPTURES THROUGH THE TEACHER

The teacher, the fifth of the fivefold callings in Ephesians 4:11, is often combined with the office of the pastor for the purpose of feeding the sheep. You cannot pastor effectively without teaching, and the only teaching that will transform hearts and change lives is the teaching of the Scriptures.

In 1990 President George H. W. Bush declared that year the "International Year of Bible Reading."[1] Our church responded and began using *The One Year Bible* as a common reading plan. Starting in January of that year, I preached from the weekly Old Testament readings on Sunday and from the New Testament readings on Wednesday. In the course of a year, I taught the entire Bible to the entire congregation. We grew spiritually by leaps and bounds.

I repeated this pattern again in 2007 with the same incredible results. People who had been in church for several years awakened to elementary Bible truths and basic Bible stories they had never even heard of.

I also began an in-house evaluation of how well our Christian school, children's ministry, television station, and every other entity of our ministry were teaching the Scriptures. I did it with urgency because I believe we are in a race against time, as we are quickly losing a generation to Bible illiteracy.

Although our "latest series" may sound relevant, if it does not use the Bible as its outline, something vital is missing. The church should be a hub of biblical knowledge where constant training and application of the Scriptures are paramount. How else will believers be transformed into Christ's image and be able to declare to the lost the validity and power of the gospel?

I took a golf lesson once, and the golf pro looked at my putting and said, "Mr. Stockstill, it is a miracle you have *ever* made a putt. I am going to work with you on the three-foot putt because it counts the same on the scorecard as a three-hundred-yard drive." In a similar fashion, too many Christians are enamored with the latest big prophetic revelation, but they can't balance their checkbooks, discipline their children, or pursue healthy dating relationships guided by biblical standards. Pastors must ingrain the example stories of the Old Testament, the simple mandates of the Gospels, and the local church standards of the Epistles into their congregations. There is no substitute.

Some would say that the average believer is uninterested in biblical things. The hectic pace of everyday life overrides whatever latent desires he or she may have for the things of God. That idea, however, was disproved to me in January of 1998 when I got involved teaching the Scriptures to the governor of Louisiana. I was in the final days of a protracted season of prayer and fasting with our church when suddenly I had an inner witness as I drove on the interstate past the Governor's Mansion. Like a flash in my spirit, I saw a picture of a wind blowing open the front door of his mansion and concluded that God was about to open a door to his office for me.

A week later, I received an unexpected call from his office. The caller told me that the governor had been on his treadmill that morning and had seen the daily ninety-second Bible program I do on secular television. An inner voice said to him,

"Call that man." He asked if I could teach him the entire Bible in four lessons!

The following week, I began my study with him, his wife, his son, and about fifteen of his executive staff. These busy people, with schedules far more packed than the average person's, were hungry to learn the Bible. After the first four lessons, the governor requested that we continue, and we did—for *six years*! I taught him and his staff every book in the Bible, either in topical or expositional form. The governor even received an associate's degree from our Bible training institute because he learned so much!

During that time, we saw miraculous answers to prayer that turned hurricanes around and brought rain on parched fields. The sheer power of the Scriptures to build the governor's faith had a profound effect on bringing Louisiana through dark economic and spiritual times during his administration.

Is it any wonder that so many Christians are hardly any different in their thoughts, speech, finances, and marriages than the unsaved? They have had no teaching and are "destroyed for lack of knowledge" (Hos. 4:6). Pastors should go through every phase, program, and event of their churches and ask this basic question: What does this do to enhance a person's understanding of the Scriptures? The activities of children's ministries, small groups, services, outreach media (television, radio, printed materials), Christian schools, and missions efforts should all answer that one question.

Believers too should examine themselves and check to see if they are spending daily time in the Word, teaching it methodically to their children, and giving it supremacy in their lives.

All of Christian life should begin and end with a deepening of that foundation.

"Faith comes by hearing, and hearing by the word of God" (Rom. 10:17, NKJV). Christians deprived of real knowledge of the Bible are doomed to fear, unbelief, and hopelessness. Ignorance of the Scriptures will leave them anemic, dysfunctional, and defeated. We must take active steps, therefore, to ensure that we hunger anew for God's Word, that we pant for it, like the deer after the water (Ps. 42:1). Then, as parents, teachers, and pastors, we must transfer that love of Scripture to a new generation of Bible-loving believers, diligently teaching them and training them in biblical knowledge.

The five dysfunctions of being unfathered, uncorrected, unfruitful, unhealed, and untaught can be remedied by reinstituting the fivefold ministry as outlined in Ephesians 4:11. When that is done, a new revival of holiness, faith, and outreach will explode.

God is raising up a new standard in America. He is raising up spiritual Nazirites who will focus on the five needs of the church. Their priorities will be right, and their code of conduct will be blameless. This code of conduct, the Ten Commandments of Ministry, helps to lay a new template, a new foundation for ministry. If enough pastors and individual Christians adopt these ten priorities, America will be shaken by their righteousness—not by their failures.

In the next chapters, walk with me through these ten values. See if the Holy Spirit will not deal with you, prune you, correct you, adjust you, and heal you. I know the day is dark and the hour is late, but America's finest hour is at hand if we, God's people, will wake up, shake ourselves, and put on our beautiful garments: "Awake, awake, clothe yourself in your strength, O Zion; clothe yourself in your beautiful garments, O Jerusalem, the holy city; for the uncircumcised and the unclean will no longer come into you" (Isa. 52:1).

QUESTIONS TO THINK ABOUT

1. What kinds of things do we sometimes use in place of private study of the Word of God? Why are none of these sufficient for maturing us in our Christian walk?

2. How do you keep the Word of God a priority in your personal spiritual life?

3. Has God ever spoken to you through His Word? What was the circumstance, and what did He say to you? Did it encourage you to dig deeper into the Word on a daily basis, or did you put your Bible down until the next time you needed something from God?

4. What is your favorite book in the Bible? Why do you like it so much? Which Bible verse more than any other sums up your life's work and vision? What makes it so special to you?

5. Take a moment and examine yourself: Do you read the Word of God daily? Do you ask the Holy Spirit to teach you as you read? Do you bring your Bible to church and follow along in your Bible as the pastor preaches, or do you just look at the verses projected onto an overhead screen? Do you study the Word for yourself, or do you depend upon your pastor to do that and then teach it to you? Are you ready to make the Scriptures a top priority in your spiritual life?

PART 2

THE TEN COMMANDMENTS OF MINISTRY

CHAPTER 6

COMMANDMENT 1: PRAYER

I want the men in every place to pray, lifting up
holy hands, without wrath and dissension.

—1 TIMOTHY 2:8

A S I WRITE THIS CHAPTER, I AM IN SEOUL, SOUTH
Korea, at the world's largest church, pastored by David
Yonggi Cho. Its vast membership of seven hundred
fifty thousand is committed to a first priority they have utilized
for fifty years in building this landmark church: the power of
prayer and fasting.

Yoido Full Gospel Church has constant prayer. From their
daily morning prayer meetings attended by thousands to the
Friday all-night prayer meetings, the flame of prayer never
goes out. Their "prayer and fasting" mountain, located about
an hour north of Seoul near the demilitarized zone with North
Korea, hosts up to thirty thousand on the weekends and
hundreds daily in small prayer grottoes where members with-
draw to pray and fast.

Yoido Full Gospel is not unique, however. Scores of prayer

mountains exist for almost every other denomination in South Korea as well. No wonder the largest church in most mainline denominations is located in Seoul!

I have been privileged to be on Dr. Cho's board of Church Growth International (CGI) for almost fourteen years. His deep humility and integrity at seventy years of age, with fifty of those years spent raising up this church from a small tent in the slums of Seoul to its present-day size, are legendary.

I remember his first visit to Bethany in April of 1993. After the evening service, he told me that he wanted to learn all he could from me! I was shocked and embarrassed by his humility, which has continued all these years.

One of the most important things I have learned from Dr. Cho is the power of prayer. In his pattern of prayer called *tabernacle prayer*, he uses the various articles of furniture in the Old Testament temple and in the heavenly temple described in Revelation as points of reference. He uses this as a model of approach to God and spends usually at least three hours a day (three times a day, for one hour each time) praying through this model. As we take a look at this first and most important commandment of ministry, let's begin with a short outline of that powerful prayer.[1]

TABERNACLE PRAYER

The brazen altar: the cross

The first thing a person noticed when entering the Old Testament tabernacle was the brazen altar. This large brass-covered "barbecue grill" was designed for a huge animal to be laid on it and consumed from beneath.

The brazen altar represents the cross. God wants our first

entrance into fellowship with Him to include gratitude for what Christ did on the cross. Every day I thank the Lord for each wound in His body and what it redeemed me from.

The laver: sanctification

Located behind the brazen altar was a birdbath-shaped object with a surface made of mirrors. As the priest began the ritualistic cleansing of his hands and feet, he looked down into this laver and saw his reflection.

Each day we should come to the laver and look realistically at ourselves in light of God's Word. His Word is a mirror, and the "washing of water by the word" (Eph. 5:26, NKJV) will cleanse our consciences.

Since we are three parts (body, mind, spirit; see 1 Thessalonians 5:23), we should submit first our bodies (hands, eyes, tongue, etc.); then our minds (pride, greed, and lust); and finally our spirits (praying for the nine fruit of the Spirit). Dr. Cho likes to take the Ten Commandments given to Moses and examine himself in terms of any idolatry, untruthfulness, hatred, or any other wrong thing he has allowed into his life. The net result of coming to the laver purifies our bodies, souls, and spirits so that we will allow no place to the devil.

The candlestick: the Holy Spirit

When a person entered the first chamber of the tabernacle, on the left stood the candlestick. Six golden branches proceeded out of a central shaft, and the light of the lamp stand was never extinguished. No other light shone in the tabernacle, and in Revelation the candlestick is identified as the "Sevenfold Spirit of God" (Rev. 4:5, THE MESSAGE).

Isaiah 11:2 describes six of the aspects of the Holy Spirit:

the spirit of wisdom and understanding, the spirit of counsel and might, and the spirit of knowledge and the fear of the Lord. The seventh aspect might be the "Spirit of the Lord," the central title of all the other six.

Every day we should ask the Holy Spirit to manifest in us His humility of wisdom, understanding of the future, counsel for decisions, power for service, knowledge of revelation, respect for holiness, and general dependence upon the Holy Spirit as Lord.

The table of shewbread: relationships

Across from the lamp stand stood a golden table with twelve loaves of fresh bread. Each loaf represented God's fellowship with His twelve tribes of Israel. Paul carried this metaphor into the New Testament: "For we, though many, are one bread and one body; for we all partake of that one bread" (1 Cor. 10:17, NKJV).

In this area of prayer, we pray for our relationships and fellowship within the body of Christ. We lift to the Lord the other members of our small group, our pastors, and other key relationships in our circle of influence. (I use the principle of twelve advocated in *The Master Plan of Evangelism* by Robert Coleman and pray for the twelve individuals I am discipling for the Lord.)

The altar of incense: worship

The altar of incense was a small, gold-covered pedestal on which a priest offered a portion of incense twice a day. This altar is also seen in heaven: "Another angel came and stood at the altar, holding a golden censer; and much incense was given to him, so that he might add it to the prayers of all the saints on the golden altar which was before the throne. And the smoke of the incense, with the prayers of the saints, went up before God out of the angel's hand" (Rev. 8:3–4).

As we approach the altar of incense, we are moving toward the final stage of our season of prayer, and it is entered into with deep, intimate worship. At this stage, I sing and worship the Lord with "psalms and hymns and spiritual songs" (Eph. 5:19). One of my favorite psalms, Psalm 23, forms the basis for worshiping the seven major divine names of Jehovah revealed in the Old Testament:

- ⤻ Jehovah-Rohi, my shepherd (v. 1): "The LORD is my shepherd."
- ⤻ Jehovah-Jireh, my provider (v. 1): "I shall not want."
- ⤻ Jehovah-Shalom, my peace (v. 2): "He makes me lie down in green pastures."
- ⤻ Jehovah-Rapha, my healer (v. 3): "He restores my soul."
- ⤻ Jehovah-Tsidkenu, my righteousness (v. 3): "He guides me in the paths of righteousness."
- ⤻ Jehovah-Shammah, my presence (v. 4): "Though I walk through the valley of the shadow of death . . . You are with me."
- ⤻ Jehovah-Nissi, my defender (v. 5): "You prepare a table before me in the presence of my enemies."

The ark of the covenant: the mercy seat

The final area of the tabernacle included the holy of holies and the ark of the covenant. There is, evidently, also an ark in heaven: "And the temple of God which is in heaven was opened; and the ark of His covenant appeared in His temple" (Rev. 11:19).

The high priest entered the holy of holies once a year to offer propitiation and to offer intercession for Israel. In a similar fashion, Paul encourages that "entreaties and prayers, petitions and thanksgivings, be made on behalf of all men, for kings and all who are in authority, so that we may lead a tranquil and quiet life in all godliness and dignity" (1 Tim. 2:1–2).

Take the opportunity in this final area of tabernacle prayer to bring your family, your city, your nation, and your world before the Lord. Job prayed for his *family* daily (Job 1:5). Jeremiah told the captives to pray for their *city* to have peace (Jer. 29:7). Paul encouraged us to pray for the leaders of our *nation* (1 Tim. 2:2). Jesus taught us to pray for the *world* harvest (Luke 10:2).

No prayer track should become a bondage; it is meant to be a blessing. A train is actually most free when on the track, and sometimes we Christians need a focal point that keeps us on track in our prayers. That is precisely what tabernacle prayer and other prayer tracks (for example, the Lord's Prayer and the prayer of Jabez) accomplish.

PRAYER AND FASTING

Prayer is energized by fasting. However, fasting can become legalistic and unfocused, as can any spiritual discipline. So, what is the point and what is the benefit of missing some meals?

The purpose of the Lord's fast is to "to loosen the bonds of wickedness, to undo the bands of the yoke, and to let the oppressed go free and break every yoke" (Isa. 58:6). Fasting is a humbling of the soul, a turning away from the things of the world and directing the spirit toward heaven.

Much has been written about fasting, but suffice it to say that the early church felt the need to fast before every leadership decision (Acts 13:2–3; 14:23). Individuals should fast for their personal hunger for God to return. Churches should fast for major breakthroughs in their ministries. Even nations should fast in times of serious trouble.

Fasting does not replace faith and does not signal spirituality. However, I have learned through the years that when I draw aside from television, media, and all the activities of eating and satisfying my flesh, my spirit begins to hear from God. Therefore, I set aside every Saturday to fast until evening. I also try to set aside the first three days of every month to seek the Lord for His blessing upon that month. In the first of the year, I spend a protracted time in fasting and usually lead our church in twenty-one days of prayer and fasting. This emphasis on systematic fasting has become a movement in America and is bringing great breakthroughs in the lives of individuals and the churches they attend.

Some people struggle with fasting because of their metabolism. I encourage them to drink juice, if necessary, to keep their metabolism operating efficiently. The point is not to punish your body, but to deny your body the control of appetites.

THE BURDEN OF PRAYER

I believe that prayer and fasting occur when we are carrying a burden for others. Paul referred to a state of heart that was never able to rest as long as his brethren were unsaved: "I am telling the truth in Christ, I am not lying, my conscience testifies with me in the Holy Spirit, that I have great sorrow and unceasing grief in my heart. For I could wish that I myself were accursed, separated from Christ for the sake of my brethren, my kinsmen according to the flesh" (Rom. 9:1–3).

How easy it is to lose that burden, that unceasing sense of concern over the state of the lost! Our hobbies, obligations, careers, and possessions distract us, even from those around us, let alone the 5 billion lost people in the world (a conservative estimate, even if 1.5 billion on Earth are believers).

If we could create a single-file line of five billion souls, how far would it reach? As a point of reference, the terrible Indonesian tsunami of December 2005 claimed two hundred fifty thousand lives, and a line of that number of lost people would reach forty miles! Amazingly enough, the line of those eternally lost would extend *forty times around the equator of the earth*! Imagine the faces of forty lines of people encircling the twenty-five-thousand-mile circumference of the earth. Feel the heart of God for those He created to spend eternity with Him in heaven, but whose destination is an eternity separated from Him.

There must be a remnant who will rise up with a burden and compassion in their spirits for the lost. Millions are being saved, but billions remain unsaved. Only those Christians who carry a prayer burden will be endlessly involved in reaching the lost, for that is the heartbeat of God.

Moses stood on the mountain with his hands uplifted as Joshua fought Amalek in the valley below (Exod. 17:11). His upraised hands brought victory, but when his hands fell to his side, it meant defeat. We are facing a crisis in our world and nation that requires us to single-mindedly focus on standing in the gap, raising our hands in intercession to a God who hears.

A burden for prayer and fasting is the foundation of all successful ministry and personal devotion. Systematic prayer, such as the pattern of the tabernacle, the topical prayer of the Lord's Prayer, and other structures of prayer, brings consistency and focus. The Holy Spirit will use these patterns to pray through us with "groanings too deep for words" (Rom. 8:26).

Set a personal plan for prayer, and mobilize your family, your small group, and your church to pursue intimacy with the Lord. The ways you can do this are endless. Some groups are starting twenty-four-hour prayer chains, believing for revival. Your plan may be different, but select something and get started in making prayer a priority in your life and in your church's life. Many books and manuals give greater detail of the *how*, but it all comes down to a continual burden for the needs of others and faith that prayer will release miracles to meet those needs.

Coupled with prayer is the second most important spiritual commandment needed to bring our nation back to God: Bible study.

QUESTIONS TO THINK ABOUT

1. Probably all Christians would say that nothing is more important than prayer. Why, then, do so many of us act as though it is an option rather than a necessity in our personal walk with the Lord? How much of a priority have you given to prayer in your life?

2. What are the advantages and what are the drawbacks in using a model of prayer, such as the Lord's Prayer or tabernacle prayer? Have you ever used a particular model to help you in your devotional time? Which model did you use, and how did it help you?

3. Explain the difference between true spiritual fasting and simply not eating food. What is the greatest breakthrough you have ever experienced as a result of fasting?

4. What causes Christians to lose their burden for the lost? What steps can they take to get that burden back?

5. How has your prayer life changed as you have grown in Christ? In what areas would you like to see improvement?

CHAPTER 7

COMMANDMENT 2: BIBLE STUDY

For the word of God is living and active and
sharper than any two-edged sword, and piercing
as far as the division of soul and spirit, of
both joints and marrow, and able to judge the
thoughts and intentions of the heart.

—HEBREWS 4:12

I N CHAPTER 5, I INTRODUCED THE TOPIC OF A
dysfunctional, untaught church. I firmly believe that Bible
study and emphasis on the Word will restore the health
and vitality of the American church. The body of Christ must
make a fresh commitment as did Paul to the Ephesian elders:
"And now I commend you to God and to the word of His grace,
which is able to build you up and to give you the inheritance
among all those who are sanctified" (Acts 20:32).

When I was an associate chaplain in college, a mouse kept
getting into our office at night. The chapel maintenance worker
brought in a small box of what I thought was rat poison. I was
concerned about having poison in our office, but he told me that

the substance was not at all harmful. He explained that it was simply a nonnutritive substance that rats crave. In fact, they love it so much that once they taste it, they will eat nothing else. They eat it and eat it, but since the "food" has no nutritional value, the rat slowly starves to death, even though he is eating.

What a picture of how the enemy deceives Christian disciples! He slyly sends clever thoughts, good advice, funny stories, and interesting doctrines to tickle their ears, and they love it. They cannot get enough of this "food," yet do not understand why they are sick, anemic, and perhaps even spiritually dead.

The writer of Hebrews was concerned with the spiritual state of those to whom he wrote: "For though by this time you ought to be teachers, you have need again for someone to teach you the elementary principles of the oracles of God, and you have come to need milk and not solid food. For everyone who partakes only of milk is not accustomed to the word of righteousness, for he is an infant. But solid food is for the mature, who because of practice have their senses trained to discern good and evil" (Heb. 5:12–14).

The devil's "rat poison" is a lack of knowledge of the true Word of God and a lack of application and transformation from that Word. The above Scripture from Hebrews speaks not only of having knowledge but also of walking in mature discernment. Many Christians have huge amounts of Bible knowledge at their fingertips, but their lifestyles show application of none of it. Where are we going wrong, and how can we make the Scriptures functional in practical, everyday life?

INTERACTION WITH THE SCRIPTURES

The era of video screens has been good for the church, lending a larger-than-life feel to a church service. In another sense, however, this technology has substituted observation for a hands-on interaction with the actual Scriptures, as congregants increasingly rely on the video screen. As a result, an entire generation is losing the knowledge of where the various books of the Bible are located because they never turn pages to find them.

Pastors must encourage their congregations to bring their Bibles to church for the purpose of constant interaction. Church members must reject laziness and complacency and use technology to supplement, not replace, the eternal Word. Every class has a textbook, and a student who shows up without it generally has to depend on others in test time. So it is with believers and their Bibles. Marking a Bible, taking notes in the margin, and finding passages in it are all parts of an interactive learning style that far supersedes mere observation.

Interaction with the Word means to handle it, hold it, make use of it, and become familiar with it. A personal Bible becomes a personal friend. Some of my earliest memories as a fervent Christian stem from when I was sixteen and the Lord called me into the ministry. Every morning at the same spot on the living room couch, I opened a King James Bible and an Amplified Bible, placing one on each leg. I compared the two, verse by verse, and marked the additional thoughts I received from the Amplified translation into the margin of my King James Bible. All my early ministry came from that intensive, daily, interactive study of the Word of God.

Now I interact with a computer Bible program. Hundreds of Bible research programs are available (some free of charge) that make *Strong's Concordance*, Bible dictionaries, Bible atlases, and good commentaries available with the click of a mouse. In addition, the Internet offers tremendous study programs so that anyone truly hungry for the Bible can learn rapidly within a basic framework of biblical understanding.

What used to take hours to study and research now takes only seconds. Within my particular Bible program are folders where I can store hundreds of Scriptures on a particular topic (guidance, covenant, marriage, etc.), which I can then call up or print out at will. I carry my computer with me worldwide, and all my research (and library) goes with me.

As wonderful as technology is and as grateful as I am for it, it can never replace the expositional, verse-by-verse method of preaching that for centuries grounded millions of believers in the Scriptures. Pastors who find a central passage for each of their sermons, rather than use endless cross-references that the average church member has a hard time keeping up with, will build a foundation of maturity in their congregations. It may not be flashy and it may not happen overnight, but pastors who methodically teach the Word, line upon line and precept upon precept, are equipping their congregations with real tools to solve their all-too-real problems.

Church members too must embrace the priority of the Word of God. *Nothing* is as powerful as a single phrase in a verse that directly applies to life. "For the Word of God is living and active and sharper than any two-edged sword" (Heb. 4:12). Dramas can be thought-provoking, solo specials are inspiring, and video presentations may be dazzling, but nothing has more power than the timeless Scriptures to change a life or mend a broken heart.

We see this dependence upon the Word of God in many, many instances of Scripture. Peter quoted a lengthy passage from the Book of Joel and three passages from Psalms in his first sermon at Pentecost (where three thousand were saved). Stephen quoted at least twelve Old Testament passages in his sermon at Jerusalem (Acts 7). Paul quoted six passages in his sermon at Pisidian Antioch (Acts 13:13). His commendation of the Bereans was that "they received the word with great eagerness, examining the Scriptures daily to see whether these things were so" (Acts 17:11). All believers need to feel totally comfortable interacting with and examining the Scriptures, not for the sake of arguing, but for godly edification.

RELEVANCE OF THE SCRIPTURES

If pastors are going to focus on getting people to interact with the Bible, they are going to have to find creative ways to relate biblical truths to what is largely a biblically illiterate generation. The most creative ideas should center upon making the Word come alive in the daily lives of the hearers. Impressive doctrinal nuances, laborious timelines, and excessive theological terminology leave most believers out in the cold. Their minds tell them, "There is no way to understand the Scriptures. I will leave that to the professionals."

In college I once saw a funny cartoon posted on the door of my major professor's office. It was taken from Matthew 16, where Jesus asks Peter, "Whom do men say I am?" The cartoon went something like this:

> **JESUS:** Whom do men say that I am?
>
> **PETER:** You are the supernatural manifestation of the ontological ground of being, a new

metaphysical rubric by which our leap of faith
is channeled into helpful societal dialectics.

JESUS: I am *who*?

"And He straightway charged him to tell no man concerning
who He was!"

My father always says, "God puts the cookies on the bottom
shelf so everyone can reach them." We may think we sound
spiritual and may feel overly impressed with ourselves for
putting our ideas and vocabulary out of the reach of the average
person, but if no one can understand our message, how will
anyone come to know Christ or have the equipment they need
to fight the enemy in their hour of crisis?

Much of the problem in preaching or even informal sharing
of the gospel comes from aiming at the "front row" instead
of the "back row." On the back row sits the family who came
in late, fought on the way to church, has an unattended child
crawling under the pew, and is trying to decide if coming to
church was really a good idea. On the front row sits the "amen
corner" of faithful churchgoers who follow every point of the
message, Bible in lap. If the message is geared to seeing that
the front row gets blessed, the message will usually fall on deaf
ears the farther back it travels. If the message aims to make the
Bible relevant and understandable to the person on the back
row, however, it will usually catch everyone in between.

Never forget that the Great Physician came for the sick, and
the Good Shepherd came for the one rather than the ninety-
nine. If you lose touch with that one thought, you'll find your
preaching and witnessing weak and watered down. It will lose

its punch while you shout hallelujah and congratulate yourself on moving in the "deeper" things of God.

My wife has had an interesting interaction with our current generation of youth by volunteering to do Bible teaching at our state correctional institute for boys. She uses Bible videos and quickly discovered that even stories like David and Goliath were totally foreign to many of the boys. She then implemented a Scripture memory component to her Saturday sessions (with candy bars awarded for success!). As they found Christ, the boys began to grow hungry for the Scriptures.

There are countless ways for ordinary believers to use the Scriptures to touch their families, neighbors, and co-workers. I'm not talking about being "preachy" or quoting a trite Bible verse every time someone shares a problem with you. People want real answers to their problems. But when you first genuinely love them, interact with them on a regular basis, and share regularly and naturally the truths found in God's Word, you might be surprised how interested they become in the God you serve and what He says in Scripture.

DEVOTION TO THE SCRIPTURES

The first believers "were continually devoting themselves to the apostles' teaching" (Acts 2:42). The devotional habit of the daily reading of Scripture is the single most important thing we must instill in believers. In chapter 5, I mentioned how our congregation is moving together through *The One Year Bible,* year after year. I punctuate their readings with messages that follow that reading plan.

Reading, however, can become a "race to the finish." I once heard an illustration of the different ways you can travel from

Baton Rouge to Los Angeles. If you go by plane, you will see a little. If you go by car, you will see a lot more. If you go by bicycle, you will see a huge amount of the countryside. But if you go by foot, you will see *everything*. The same is true of the reading of Scripture: the slower you move, the more you see.

This does not mean that a surface reading of the stories, history, and characters in the Bible is bad in itself. Everyone should make a first pass through *The One Year Bible* or some other yearly reading plan. However, it is the observation and application of Scripture that bring life. Journaling relevant thoughts and teaching moments that come through the reading of the Word is also very helpful.

All my preaching comes out of the "walk to Los Angeles" approach. No matter how many times I have read the Bible through (perhaps fifty to sixty times now), I see something totally fresh and new every day. As I read, I meditate on a verse until a *rhema* word comes into my spirit. A *rhema* (a Greek term generally used for a specific, revealed word as opposed to a *logos* word, which is general and objective) is what Paul refers to as "the sword of the Spirit, which is the word [*rhema*] of God" (Eph. 6:17). Additionally, Jesus said, "Man shall not live on bread alone, but on every word [*rhema*] that proceeds out of the mouth of God" (Matt. 4:4). When believers understand that daily reading from God's Word gives them fresh manna from heaven for their circumstances, they will become totally devoted to Bible reading.

Devotion to the Scriptures also means a refusal to deviate from the Scriptures. How many "rabbit trails" and outright heresies exist because someone is "peddling the word of God" (2 Cor. 2:17) and "adulterating the word of God" (2 Cor. 4:2)?

I once heard a great Scottish preacher say, "It is not just what Scripture *says*, but what Scripture *also says*." To build doctrine and dogma on a single sliver of out-of-context Scripture is the craft of the heretic's art. The "Word in balance" is a watchword for maintaining the general body of thought the Spirit is communicating through the Scriptures rather than espousing a "revelation" that will tickle the ears but has no solid footing. Remember the "eighty-eight reasons Christ must come in 1988" book that sold thousands of copies—until 1989, that is? Stay on guard against such things.

When I was a missionary in Ghana in 1976, we started a poultry farm to supplement our operating budget (bad idea, by the way). We did not know that the country was so poor that it had no poultry vaccines. In one night, a chicken virus went through our farm, and in the morning a thousand chickens lay dead. I think of that picture in my mind often as I see the "chicken viruses" of unbalanced teachings and stretched semantics bringing down thousands of believers across our nation today. "To the law and to the testimony! If they do not speak according to this word, it is because they have no dawn," said Isaiah of the false prophets and charlatans in his day (Isa. 8:20).

Interaction, relevancy, and devotion to the Scriptures must come front and center in the American church. Rather than seeking to disguise biblical concepts, we should promote the actual words of Scripture through expositional preaching. Believers should interact with their Bibles in their daily prayer time, do personal interactive study with study tools or computers, and become biblically fluent in order to train their children. As the Scriptures say, "This book of the law shall not depart from your mouth, but you shall meditate on it day and night" (Josh. 1:8). "These words...shall be on your heart. You shall teach them diligently to your sons and shall talk of them when you sit in your house and when you walk by your way and when you lie down and when you rise up" (Deut. 6:6–7).

Through the power of prayer and fasting and powerful Bible study and preaching, we will bring a great revival to America. Now we are ready to move into another great area of restoration that must happen in the American church: the return of integrity.

QUESTIONS TO THINK ABOUT

1. What are some specific ways that the Word of God has had an impact in your life? What truths do you know now that you did not know before you became knowledgeable of the Word? What is the most life-changing revelation you ever received from the Word of God?

2. James says that we must be doers of the Word and not hearers only. How has the Word of God challenged you to put feet to your faith? In what specific area has the Word stirred your heart to do something for the kingdom? Have you done it?

3. What type of environment have you found most conducive to the reading of God's Word? What kinds of things distract you, and how do you deal with them?

4. What is the difference between the *logos* word and a *rhema* word? Which takes preeminence over the other? Have you ever known someone whose supposed *rhema* word was "off"? How does the *logos* word provide protection in this area?

5. How can we emphasize the Word and make it real to our children?

CHAPTER 8

COMMANDMENT 3: INTEGRITY

Choose a good reputation over great riches, for
being held in high esteem is better than having
silver or gold.

—PROVERBS 22:1, NLT

A BURDEN FOR THE LOST MANIFESTED IN PRAYER
and fasting coupled with the preaching of the Scripture
is the foundation of all ministry. Upon those two tenets
rests the corner pillar of success: integrity.

In math, a whole number is called an integer. Nothing
is missing, and it is totally complete. It is not three-fourths
complete or any other fractional part; it is whole. In ministry,
to have integrity means to be whole and sound (notice the
common root with the word *integer*). Ministerial integrity thus
inspires confidence, much as money does in the economic
realm. Anything less than 100 percent integrity in ministry
breeds mistrust and creates a suspicion of being robbed.

There are four areas in any Christian's life, but especially
in the ministry, that must be sound: *finances, commitments,*

honesty, and *doctrine*. Careful attention to these areas is crucial and will pay off in a lifetime of influence.

Integrity in these areas gives us a good report (reputation) in the community where we live, work, and minister. Without integrity, we have no chance to infiltrate the lost world and exert massive influence for God's kingdom.

As you read this chapter, keep in mind that though I am emphasizing ministerial integrity, the principles are applicable to all. God does not have a double standard; what He expects of the pastor in a position of visibility, He also expects of the ordinary believer. We are all ambassadors for Christ, we are all priests in His kingdom, and we all must uphold only the highest standards of integrity in our public and private lives. But because so much scandal has rocked the Christian world concerning ministerial integrity, let's take a closer look at that angle.

INTEGRITY IN FINANCES

No issue has been more scrutinized than the church's managing of its finances. Whether queries arise from the IRS, the deacon board, the U.S. Senate, the media, vendors, lawyers for former employees, or the general population, financial impropriety means instant loss of credibility. Money is so potentially dangerous that, though ministers cannot be paranoid, they must handle it as they would explosives.

In managing a church's finances, there are several basic principles to guide us and certain practical rules to protect us. If you are a pastor, check to see how well you are implementing these, and if you are a church member, use these as guidelines to help you make sound judgments concerning the local church with which you are affiliated.

1. "Owe nothing to anyone except to love one another" (Rom. 13:8).

Debt that is secured (has property standing for its value) is acceptable but still requires prompt, no-excuses repayment. Some ministries hold their payments to vendors and creditors for ninety days for cash-management purposes. At Bethany, we *never* do that, choosing rather to pay in the month we owe. That way we protect our reputation and maintain open doors to our vendors and creditors. The phrase "The check is in the mail" has become a farce. It has no place in Christian ministry.

A local ABC affiliate television station in Baton Rouge with whom we have had a good, long-standing relationship once honored our leadership team with a luncheon at their station. The owner of the station also owns the local newspaper and heads *the* media family in our city, so the luncheon was quite an honor. The station explained the reason for this beautiful luncheon with one sentence: "You are the only people on our station who have paid their bills on time for the entire twenty years your ninety-second morning program has been on."

2. The cost of buildings and their operation should never exceed 35 percent of a church's income.

Salaries should run between 20 and 40 percent. Missions giving must never fall below a tithe level of 10 percent and can increase to 25 percent or even more if the church is debt free. Savings should be 5–10 percent. These percentages do not affect integrity unless the church violates them and can no longer pay its obligations in the month they are due.

3. Money given *must* be used for the purpose designated.

There is no compromise on this principle—to do so is both illegal and unappreciated. When a member sacrifices to plant a church, build a nursery, or support a widow, those funds in the exact amount and at the time given must make their way to that need (regardless of how desperately they may be needed elsewhere).

4. Outside business interests between *leadership* and *membership* change the relationship and cannot exist.

When a pastor or church leader enters into a business relationship with a member, the relationship changes from pastor/sheep to partner/partner. Any shift in the balance of profit or responsibilities will likely bring a rift between the two.

The body of Christ is not a convenient collection of contacts. It is a holy family moving toward heaven together. Second Timothy 2:4 says, "No soldier in active service entangles himself in the affairs of everyday life, so that he may please the one who enlisted him as a soldier." I cannot see the apostle Paul with multilevel contacts in all the churches he founded. His motives remained pure because the sheep were his stewardship, not his reward.

5. Churches should adequately support their pastors and leaders: "You shall not muzzle the ox while he is threshing" (1 Cor. 9:9; see also verses 10–14).

Resources are available that post the median salary for nonprofit ministries in America. A board or congregation can proudly provide for their leadership without portraying extravagance to the watching world. Ministers are not hirelings but guardians of the flock and deserve adequate compensation. It is not the duty of the congregation to keep the pastor poor and "dependent on God." Neither is it the congregation's duty to support a lavish, extravagant lifestyle for a pastor who wants to live far above the norm.

6. Pressure for finances yields the perception of manipulation and insincerity.

It does take money to operate ministry and expand it. However, when the sheep sense that they are a means to an end, part of an agenda that equates their worth with their money, a loss of integrity results. Anyone may be accused of that, but leaders must know that they have not moved into the flesh on a project that they desire more than the Holy Spirit or the people desire. A building, a relocation, or a certain outreach must be fueled by the people's desire (like Moses's tabernacle when he had to restrain the people from giving).

7. Members deserve to be informed of expenditures.

At Bethany, we issue a financial statement at the end of each year, showing in categories all expenses and income. This is not for the purpose of budget battles, but to assure our members of our priorities (missions, youth and children, local outreach) and also our obligations (principal payments, utility costs, staff costs). We avoid listing each employee's salary because that inevitably leads to contention and strife within the staff and within the church. All our executive-level salaries are controlled by an outside compensation committee as mandated by the IRS.

COMMITMENTS

A commitment occurs when someone perceives that you have promised something. Granted, some pushy people may interpret your silence or your head bobbing up and down during their proposal as a commitment. However, a real commitment is not a misunderstanding, but a genuine obligation you make in good faith.

"Your word is your bond" was the maxim that enabled my grandfather to borrow money at a local bank in the 1930s with only a handshake. That was a time when a man would rather die than break his word.

The Bible declares that a man of integrity "swears to his own hurt and does not change" (Ps. 15:4). When a commitment comes out of your mouth, you must have the same integrity with it that God has to His Word. You would be better off to bear personal expense rather than change a commitment you publicly made.

Commitments from the pulpit, of course, are inviolate. Our staff knows that if I announce something to the people, it becomes our new direction. It takes only once for a pastor to alter his word to bring suspicion of any and every announcement. Of course, mistakes may be made, but if the pastor has set a course, he must follow through. This brings confidence in the pulpit as the true source of accurate information about the direction of the church.

Individual commitments by church members are just as sacred. When you say you will work in the nursery for the next quarter, but after two weeks claim God "told" you to quit, you are breaking your commitment. When you pledge a certain amount to the new building program but decide to instead use the money for a "much-deserved" vacation, you are violating a commitment. Just as you depend upon the church's leaders to keep their word to you, they are counting on you to do what you promise.

Samuel lived an open life before the nation. His final speech showed his integrity: "'Here I am; bear witness against me before the Lord and His anointed. Whose ox have I taken, or whose donkey have I taken, or whom have I defrauded? Whom have I oppressed, or from whose hand have I taken a bribe to blind my eyes with it? I will restore it to you.' They said, 'You have not defrauded us or oppressed us or taken anything from any man's hand'" (1 Sam. 12:3–4). Oh, that the same could be said about all of us!

Commitments also involve the area of responsibilities. Before you accept a responsibility, you should count the cost. (See Luke 14:28.) To commit to something means to shift your weight to a point where it cannot be reversed. Stay with your commitments until completed. Don't commit to an event, a project, a board, or a task and then change your mind about it. Christian believers and leaders must exhibit the steadiest, most trustworthy commitments in the community.

Sadly, pastors sometimes cancel international missionary commitments because of their distant and anonymous nature. Promised crusades, conferences, and building projects disappear because of budget restraints or because "the Lord has moved in a different direction." Additionally, emotionally charged church members during missions conventions sometimes make pledges to support certain missionaries on a monthly basis, only to never give even the first month's support.

One of our national pastors in Nigeria once hitchhiked

and walked for over a month across the entire continent of Africa just to attend a conference in Kenya. When he reached Nairobi, he discovered the sponsoring American ministry had suddenly canceled. He hitchhiked and walked back home but never did understand what had happened.

Having been a missionary in Africa for almost two years, I have since picked up the brokenhearted pieces that come when pastors and individuals fail to follow through with their missionary commitments. When I commit to supporting a missionary for a year, I would rather forgo my own salary than send that person to the field and leave him or her hanging.

But that is exactly what happens too many times. Many missionaries tell me stories of pastors and individual Christians who promise them support for a year but stop after two months. Missionaries have just come to expect a lack of integrity in commitments made to them, thinking, "We'll believe it when we see it."

Christians, whether pastors or laypersons, should never need a legal contract to make them keep their word. If they fear the Lord and believe integrity is their highest honor, they'll willingly keep their commitments. "A good name is to be more desired than great wealth. Favor is better than silver and gold" (Prov. 22:1).

As I write this chapter on a plane coming home from Germany, I can't stop weeping. I feel such an anointing of the Holy Spirit on what I am telling you right now. Let's get it together, brothers and sisters! It's time for a new standard of integrity that no worldly institution can even begin to rival. The reputation of not only the American church but also our

Savior Himself is at stake, and we must radically change direction and dedicate ourselves to keeping our commitments.

HONESTY

In a court of law, you are asked, "Do you promise to tell the truth, the whole truth, and nothing but the truth?" Integrity means a commitment to the entire truth. It is following the scriptural mandate to "provide things honest in the sight of all men" (Rom. 12:17, KJV).

If you leave out pertinent facts (selective amnesia) in an effort to persuade, it is a lie. A lie is simply any intent to deceive. Therefore, lies are not only what you say but also what you allow people to believe for untruthful purposes. *This is an important word.* Intentionally withholding pertinent truth that leads people to wrong conclusions does not show integrity.

Exaggeration is another serious temptation in the honesty area. Someone defined honesty as the "accurate recollection of facts." One person ministered in our church years ago and described a bus he was using to transport cancer patients. My father calculated the length the bus would have to be in order to hold the number of people the minister said it could hold. That bus would have needed to be over 125 feet long! When confronted with this obvious inaccuracy, the minister responded, "You know, you can't tell anything too big for God."

This pitiful response reminds us that testimonies of miracles, answered prayer, and apparent supernatural interventions must be accurate. God does not need any help defending His greatness. It diminishes His glory when certain facts come out later that cast a shadow over the truthfulness of a miracle.

Fear of embarrassment also brings a great temptation to

be dishonest. When failures and flaws become obvious, the crisis passes the moment the truth is told. People can adjust to reality, but not to a sense of denial. As embarrassing as the truth may be, when you tell the "truth, the whole truth, and nothing but the truth," the crisis ends.

The world expects truthfulness from its leaders: athletes, politicians, actors, and, yes, even spiritual leaders. Christians, more than any other group of people, must lead the way in becoming known as those who have nothing to hide and whose self-disclosure is legendary. The world is indeed watching.

The root of all dishonesty is *pride* and *insecurity*. Those who appear shady, slippery, and devious have a deep sense of insecurity that they will be rejected if their faults are known. But there's an answer to that problem: just admit it! Bring your pride to the cross and be transparent. People will not reject you; they will respect you. The greatest Christians I know are totally transparent with others and are greatly loved in return for this confirmation that we are all, indeed, just flesh.

DOCTRINE

I have included this topic under integrity because Scripture often refers to doctrine as something that needs to be *sound*. Second Timothy 4:3 says, "For the time will come when they will not endure sound doctrine." Titus 1:9, in speaking of overseers in the church, says that they must be able to "exhort in sound doctrine," and Titus 2:1 exhorts us to "speak the things which are fitting for sound doctrine."

Shady, flaky doctrine built upon a wisp of revelation hurts the credibility of the body of Christ. That kind of doctrine may tickle the itching ears of some who long for something novel, but in the long run it destroys. A ministry that will stretch Scripture to fit its agenda reminds me of the ancient Egyptian king who forced his guests to fit the bed, stretching them to fit if they were too short and cutting off their feet if they were too long. That is unbelievably ridiculous, and so is it when we stretch the Scriptures.

Without being irreverent to what some hold dear, I must state that espousing doctrines that radically alter wholesome community behavior hurts our integrity. Snake handling (based on Mark 16:18), never-die-ism (based on John 11:26), or refusal to seek medical attention based on an isolated verse borders on presumption, not faith.

Your doctrine needs to be sound. This means having balance, holding to a solid thread of scriptural truth that runs throughout the Bible, and not building on a nuance of Greek or Hebrew inflection in *Strong's Concordance.* Predictions, time lines, and scriptural "facts" that are mere interpretations shake people's faith when the predictions don't come true. Many were convinced "scripturally" that Anwar Sadat was the Antichrist—until he was assassinated! Preface your particular insight into Bible doctrine with a qualifier such as, "It is possible that…" and avoid dogmatic statements like, "This obviously means…"

As we move into perilous times, more and more I am becoming a stickler for sound footing on any and every doctrine. You will not be penalized in your effectiveness for the Lord by not adopting the latest doctrinal fad. You *will* be penalized if you catch each doctrinal "flu bug" that comes around and then "recover." Your soundness and integrity will come into question.

The relics of the doctrinal fancies of the last forty years litter the evangelical landscape like old cars in derelict junkyards. If a new idea surfaces, think of that doctrine's history, beginning in the early church with the church fathers. Perhaps it is an old, recycled deception that our forefathers bled and died to correct.

My father-in-law once made a statement that has guided me in these areas of integrity discussed in this chapter. He said, "Integrity is like virginity. When it's gone, it's gone." Truly your finances, commitments, honesty, and doctrine form the essence of your good name.

Paul told Timothy, "Retain the standard of sound words which you have heard from me, in the faith and love which are in Christ Jesus. Guard, through the Holy Spirit who dwells in us, the treasure which has been entrusted to you" (2 Tim. 1:13–14). Satan would give anything to steal your treasure, so you must guard it. If you fail, honestly admit it and change immediately. Your family, your church, and the gospel are depending on it.

Related to integrity is another huge area where God commands us to walk with honor: purity.

QUESTIONS TO THINK ABOUT

1. How does the way you handle your finances reveal your heart? Why do you think so few Christians live significantly different lifestyles from their unsaved neighbors and friends when it comes to their financial choices?

2. What kind of debt, if any, is acceptable for a Christian or a church? Under what circumstances, if any, is credit-card debt allowable? Why do you think so few people or churches make freedom from debt a high priority? Have you made it a priority in your life?

3. What kinds of excuses do people give for failing to keep their commitments? Is there ever a legitimate reason to not keep a commitment you have made?

4. A lie is any intent to deceive; it includes acts of omission as well as acts of commission. When you consider this broader definition for deception, what kinds of behavior do we sometimes engage in that really are deceptive? How does it tarnish God's reputation when His people exaggerate His exploits or cover up known wrongdoing?

5. How can you know if your doctrine is sound? What should you do if you are in a church that preaches questionable doctrine?

CHAPTER 9

COMMANDMENT 4: PURITY

The wisdom from above is first pure.

—JAMES 3:17

OUR MORAL VALUES ARE IN FREE FALL. *PURITY* HAS become a laughable term. Roving eyes spot bare flesh anywhere it is exposed. Elaborate cover-ups are revealed for all to see on *Cheaters*. Men with impeccable records astonish the public with their secret indulgences.

None of these trends strike with more shock value than when found in ministry. Each exposure hardens the American soul to the gospel as the legendary purity of people like Billy Graham is passing from the scene.

I once heard a story that Billy Graham's team inspected his hotel room each evening before he retired, looking under the bed and in the closet to make sure no one had planted a female to bring a false accusation against him. I don't know if that story is true, but what is true is that Billy Graham's many years of ministerial purity and marital faithfulness loom like Gibraltar in the American conscience.

We Christians, and especially pastors, have to get our acts together. There will always be failures in the area of moral purity, but surely we can stem the tide. Surely there can be more of us who, many years down the road, can lay claim to long-term moral purity, men like my father, who has upheld purity in his life and ministry for sixty-three years now.

The mother of a friend of mine lived out in the country. For years this woman carried a flyswatter in her home so she could kill the flies that constantly flew in through the open windows. Finally, her son suggested she put screens on the windows. Screens don't guarantee a "no-fly" environment, but they can sure cut down on the number that do get in!

Though we cannot guarantee moral purity, there are actions we can take to filter out impurity. There are certain precautions and standards we can abide by to preclude the constant news of yet another Christian businessman, minister, or leader in a runaway affair. Who, besides me, is ready for a radical, routine standard of purity?

Purity is the Christian's generational legacy, but impurity will stain your life forever, as it did for David, Israel's great king, and affect the generations that come after you. Let's see what purity is and how we can maintain it.

WHAT IS PURITY?

Purity refers to the inward control of fleshly lusts, thoughts, and actions. It means "unmixed," a state of being without compromise. It means "uncontaminated," free from outside corruption. Isn't it interesting that something pure is called "unadulterated"? We desperately need some unadulterated Christians!

Paul said, "To the pure, all things are pure; but to those who are defiled and unbelieving, nothing is pure, but both their mind and their conscience are defiled" (Titus 1:15). My thoughts go back to the Nazirites, whose standing before God depended on their purity. To touch a dead body, partake of the grape, or cut their hair meant defilement from the highest position of holiness. Samuel, Samson, and John the Baptist were lifetime Nazirites, men dedicated to God from their births.

Samson, unfortunately, illustrates the lack of purity we often find in the body of Christ. His little compromises paved the way for his big collapse. It is the "little foxes that spoil the vines" (Song of Sol. 2:15, NKJV), and we see a pattern of that in Samson's ministry. In Judges 14:5, a lion jumped him in the vineyard, but have you ever wondered why he was in the vineyard to begin with (where there are grapes)? What was he doing that he felt compelled to hide from his parents (v. 6)? Why did he later touch the dead carcass of the lion to get some honey (vv. 8–9), when he had been forbidden to touch anything dead? And, ultimately, why did he ever reveal to Delilah the source of his strength? Like a moth drawn to a candle, he flirted with impurity and compromise.

I once heard a good illustration of this dangerous flirting with sin. A deadly coral reef can lurk right below the surface of a body of water. Unseen in a channel, such a reef can rip the bow of a ship in half and sink it in a minute. What if you were passing through a channel that had coral reefs on both sides? Would you see how close you could get to either reef without touching it? Or would you steer down the middle of the channel to be absolutely sure you didn't get near either one?

Samson played the odds and lost. The other two lifetime

Nazirites, Samuel and John the Baptist, kept themselves pure and enjoyed increased influence throughout their lifetimes.

We must make it our highest priority to walk in purity. Jesus said, "Blessed are the pure in heart, for they shall see God" (Matt. 5:8). Without purity, no one will see the Lord because God is totally pure. In the Old Testament, purification came through the sprinkling of blood and water. In the New Testament, it comes through applying the blood of Jesus to our minds and spirits: "Let us draw near with a sincere heart in full assurance of faith, having our hearts sprinkled clean from an evil conscience and our bodies washed with pure water" (Heb. 10:22).

Even in the natural world, we desire purity. Our bodies long to breathe pure air and drink pure water. Whole Foods supermarket has made millions marketing food that is free from preservatives and additives. (Someone suggested calling it Whole Paycheck!) People will pay any price for purity. In the spiritual world, purity is first a state of mind that is unmixed, uncontaminated, and uncondemned. Our souls and consciences long for it, like spiritual oxygen.

The Old Testament priesthood required elaborate rites of purification: "our bodies washed with pure water" (Heb. 10:22). Every particle of defilement from dirt, disease, or decomposition had to be removed to maintain an environment of worship. We know that today we are free from the law's rigors, but what is wrong with having minds and consciences that are equally pure?

PURITY IN MORALITY

The Word of God gives a clear standard for moral purity: "Or do you not know that the unrighteous will not inherit the kingdom of God? Do not be deceived; neither fornicators, nor idolaters, nor adulterers, nor effeminate, nor homosexuals, nor thieves, nor the covetous, nor drunkards, nor revilers, nor swindlers, will inherit the kingdom of God. Such were some of you; but you were washed, but you were sanctified, but you were justified in the name of the Lord Jesus Christ and in the Spirit of our God" (1 Cor. 6:9–11).

God created Adam and Eve with pure sexual desires. Their natural attraction for each other gave rise to deep intimacy and relationship. They were one in spirit first and then in body. Satan hates this powerful union and has sought from the beginning of time to pervert and disrupt God's pattern. Homosexuality, fornication, and pornography are examples of immoral behavior. Our consciences tell us these things are immoral, but Satan deceives us into thinking they are normal and acceptable.

I realize in calling these things out I am opposing a very powerful demonic spirit that has worked relentlessly to convince the American church that the things Paul called immoral are normal. We have heard the explanations of genetics, the testimonies of "successful" divorces, and the doctrinal explanations of legalism. I even had one lesbian "minister" tell me that the sin of Sodom and Gomorrah was the sin of inhospitality, not immorality! She and those like her say that it is we who uphold the obvious biblical standards who are the problem; they say our straightlaced legalism has brought condemnation on those helplessly trapped in their own bodies.

I don't believe God will be swayed by these arguments. After all, He has always been the most adamant about how things are supposed to work in the moral arena. We had better stop trying to second-guess Him and just submit to Him. He is our Creator and would never create us with uncontrollable passions that are against His Word.

PURITY IN THOUGHTS

To be honest, all impurity starts with a *thought*: "Has God said…?" (Gen. 3:1). Satan questions God's clear commands and blames Him for making the command in the first place. Paul called these kinds of thoughts "high things" (2 Cor. 10:5, NKJV), a direct challenge from the enemy to God's revealed standard. If thoughts, then, are the problem, how can we control them?

Imagine the following scenario: You are sitting alone in an airport concourse in another city. Suddenly the thought enters your mind that no one who knows you is around. Less than fifty yards away, magazine racks full of pictures of undressed women wait to be explored. To make matters worse, carelessly exposed women sit all around you, arousing your senses.

The initial thought of anonymity leads to a high thought: "Looking at a couple of pictures is better than committing adultery. After all, God made the female anatomy. It's just a silly little indulgence…" And the thoughts roll in. The high thought now begins to rule the fantasies of your mind and blocks out everything else. Finally, you obey your flesh and take a shameful action. You have a quick bout with your stricken conscience and exercise some form of repentance. As sincere as that may be, it does not remove the images, thoughts, or the knowledge that you did pull it off without consequence.

Now comes the even easier way to indulge yourself through the Internet. Your fantasy world spins out of control as you go online and become fascinated without the slightest fear of reprehension. The thought has now become a *stronghold*

(2 Cor. 10:4, NKJV). Lust has been conceived and brought forth sin, and sin is maturing and bringing forth death (James 1:15). That's exactly what happened to David with Bathsheba. If only he had not viewed her from his rooftop, his downward spiral would never have begun.

I have learned the power of the Holy Spirit within me to control lust. My body is His temple (1 Cor. 6:19), and He stands ready to spring into action on my behalf against lustful thoughts. I simply call on His name ("Holy Spirit!") under my breath the moment any impure image or thought enters my consciousness. It is amazing how quickly He extinguishes the passion and thought, much like a water pistol dousing a candle's flame.

It is quite impossible in today's world not to see images, exposures, and "opportunities" in the mall or even the church. But by making the Holy Spirit your constant filter and helper, you *can* have self-control over the lusts of the flesh that activate through inflaming thoughts.

Satan's arsenal for injecting lustful thoughts increases daily: Internet, television, newspapers, magazines, and now even telephone (soon, I'm told, to be the largest carrier of pornography). Peter, however, said to "stir up your pure minds" (2 Pet. 3:1, NKJV). And Paul said, "Whatever is pure…dwell on these things" (Phil. 4:8).

Consciously entertaining mental filth is much like allowing a garbage truck to back up to your beautiful front yard and unload. I would be outraged if that happened, and I am outraged when mail carriers unwittingly deliver soft porn to my door in the form of magazines and advertisements. I don't put up with it, and neither should you.

A few years ago, America was horrified by a Super Bowl halftime "exposure." My two teenage sons and I felt violated. It's no wonder a whole new generation of youth is battling lust like no other generation in history. It's up to us to jump into the battle with them and show them the way to moral purity.

At the moment, the Internet represents the biggest challenge to moral purity. There are, however, Internet filters that work, and I require filters on every laptop and stand-alone computer our church staff has access to. Filters may make your surfing slower and more cumbersome, but you will never face the horror of accessing unsolicited pornography because you misspelled a favorite site. I realize, of course, that having a filter, in itself, does not guarantee you won't enter the filthy world of the Internet. It does, however, keep you from entering it *accidentally*, the precursor to taking many trips there in your mind.

In a men's meeting at our church years ago, Dr. Edwin Louis Cole related the story of a man in Dallas who was part of a small group of men with whom he met weekly for accountability and fellowship. The man secretly began a relationship on the Internet with a woman in New England. When he disappeared one day to meet her, his friends looked on his computer and found where the woman lived. So great was the concern of his friends that they boarded a plane and flew to the city where he had gone. After arriving, they called his cell phone and located him. Responding to their love, the man allowed them to pray for his deliverance, bring him home, and help him reunite with his family. Though his story had a glorious ending, most stories of men captured by a sexual relationship or fantasy, unfortunately, do not end as well.

I know a good missionary couple, for example, who divorced

because of a moral failure in the husband. The wife recalled the time they were parked in their travel trailer on the way back to the mission field. She missed her husband for a few minutes and went outside to find him. She discovered him on the back side of the trailer, staring at an X-rated drive-in movie right next door. She startled him, and he apologized. Soon after, however, he cultivated a sexual relationship with a young woman in their ministry and left his wife. The seed was planted in that moment of accidental exposure: *wrong parking lot at the wrong time.* Always remember, the Internet is a constant drive-in movie, just waiting to snare your mind.

Purity in Marriage

The best defense is a good offense. You have heard that said many times, but in purity it is the guiding principle God has ordained. He said it this way: "Let your fountain be blessed, and rejoice in the wife of your youth. As a loving hind and a graceful doe, let her breasts satisfy you at all times; be exhilarated always with her love. For why should you, my son, be exhilarated with an adulteress and embrace the bosom of a foreigner?" (Prov. 5:18–20).

I understand that by revering and honoring my wife, every other sexual temptation seems trashy. My wife, Melanie, has been faithful in raising our six children: eight loads of clothes a day, innumerable meals and shopping trips, and years of homework and homeschooling. She has literally invested her life, beauty, and strength in serving my children and me. Her physical beauty that attracted me initially is still intact. Her emotional stability has matured and become regal through the years. Her wisdom in discernment, finances, personnel, and revelation is unmatched. Why would my eyes be attracted to some other woman who has her own slew of megaproblems that lie undiscovered beneath the veneer of batting eyelashes?

I choose Melanie. How in the world do men who once felt the same about their wives slip into the fantasy world of having an affair with someone else? Dr. James Dobson describes it this way: First, it starts with a *look*. When eyes meet, sparks fly. A look can become a stare. This is where adultery begins. The look, when contemplated, becomes a *touch*. A graze of the hand, a touch on the shoulder, and the chemistry rises to another level. This is definitely out of bounds for any Christian. After a few times of touch, a moment of concealed privacy leads to an *embrace*. This is where full-blown adultery is imminent. An embrace becomes a *kiss*, and the rest is obvious.[1]

Be discerning. Satan can make anything look good. If you forsake the spouse of your youth for a newer model, you will eventually discover the new person's unflattering attitudes and faults. And the same seductiveness that snagged you may very well be used to lure yet another person at another point in time!

The Book of Proverbs describes the primrose path of foolishness that leads away from reason to reprobation (Prov. 7:6–23). I feel that there is only one way to preclude a disastrous affair: accountability.

SOME PURITY RECOMMENDATIONS

I have adopted some rather stringent policies for myself that have steered me right all these years. You might want to consider them too.

1. Never be alone with someone of the opposite sex who is not your spouse.

This includes lunches, counseling, car trips, and, of course, out-of-town travel. Leave the office door open if you are meeting with or counseling a member of the opposite sex. I know this seems archaic in our modern professional world, but no amount of reasoning can lay to rest the appearance of evil you portray in any of these scenarios (not to mention how relationships blossom in privacy). Female members who want to speak to me in the lobby after service have my assistant in on the conversation, or it doesn't happen. The bottom line is to forestall any possible accusation by asking yourself, "How would I defend myself if accused by someone in this situation?"

2. Always be accountable.

My staff, my wife, and usually my personal assistant (who travels with me) are always aware of my whereabouts. I have no occasions where I am out of pocket for any period of time. (I figure that anyone wanting to bring a false accusation against me would not know my schedule well enough to construct a case.) Your spouse should never be surprised that you were in an area of town he or she did not expect you to be in. Your daily plans, schedules, and events should be an open book.

3. At work or in the church, have your IT director install and maintain the password to your Internet filter. At home, have a filter on all computers and allow only one person (probably the wife) to have the password to the account.

There are many good filters to select from. Some programs send out an e-mail to five preselected e-mail addresses if a pornographic site is viewed (with the site name attached). At work or in a church setting, the IT director should also have total access to check site histories and do regular laptop maintenance with no prior notice.

The same diligence must be exercised at home. You are fooling yourself if you think, "I don't need a filter; neither I nor the kids would ever look at such disgusting material." You don't know what you might do if given the chance, and you certainly don't know what your impressionable children will do. Installing a filter puts out the fire before it has a chance to burn. It's a safety precaution you can't afford to be without.

I'll take this one step further. Monitor closely what your children are doing on the computer. If you have a family computer, keep it in an open, visible area. Govern the times and conditions under which your children can use it. Be cautious about giving a child a laptop to use privately in his or her room. Pay attention to what your child is doing on the computer, especially if you allow him or her access to the interactive sites and chat rooms that are so popular with young people these days.

4. Travel with a partner if at all possible (one of your children, an assistant, a trusted friend, or your spouse, best of all).

I once had my daughter with me overseas when a prostitute knocked on my door in the middle of the night and was rebuffed by my daughter! I determined then and there to never travel alone. No wonder Paul and Silas traveled together.

If you are a businessperson required to often travel out of town, be on guard to Satan's temptations. Remember, standards of purity remain the same, whether at home or in a faraway location; you are never on vacation from morality. Be especially diligent to let your spouse know your schedule and where-abouts, and when possible, bring your spouse along. If that is not possible, talk daily to your spouse and keep in touch with what is going on at home while you are gone. You'll find it much easier to combat even a fleeting temptation when you stay near the home fire in your thoughts when not present in body.

5. Never allow a person of the opposite sex to share intimate feelings, dreams, or secrets with you in person or by letter.

For many of us, the workplace has replaced the neighbor-hood as the source of most of our close friendships. Though most of us must interact with the opposite sex in our work responsibilities, proper boundaries must be maintained. Keep conversation on a professional level, even when discussing casual personal details. If a co-worker of the opposite sex wants to pour out his or her heart to you, gently steer the person to a more suitable listener. Make it a matter of prayer, but don't become their confidant.

If you are a pastor, the same rules apply. Yes, you must counsel and care for the sheep, but you can't allow the bonding that takes place when people of the opposite sex share deep joy or pain. That's why, whenever possible, it is often preferable for women to counsel women and men to counsel men.

6. Notify the post office to prevent the delivery to your home of any soft porn catalogs that show scantily clad women.

They have provision to do that, and it also protects your children's vulnerable passions. Remember, what you feast the eyes upon, even accidentally, enters the brain and creates a memory—good or bad. If anything and everything is coming across your doorstep, you're allowing images in that will sear themselves into your brain and be difficult to expel. Be proactive and stop the process at the beginning before it creates a stronghold in your mind or the minds of your impressionable children.

7. Block any television sites that carry explicit movies, commercials, and programs: MTV, E!, VH1, and others.

Usually the woman in the household is the best one to control the password for the adult supervision part of your cable programming. In addition, make quality decisions about which programs are allowed and which ones are not, and then enforce them. The younger your children, the more you must supervise the quality and quantity of what they watch on TV. If in doubt about any program, don't watch it! Just because everyone else—even other Christians—is watching, it is no reason to watch it too. You answer to the Lord for your choices, the same as they do.

8. Avoid R-rated movies.

Any movies rated R could be carrying nudity. Stick with PG, and even then check out Web sites that give a heads-up on any potentially offensive scenes.

The standard for movies is the same as the standard for TV. Be selective, set the standard too high rather than too low, and if in doubt, don't watch it. You'll never regret not watching a movie or television program that might be objectionable, but you may very well regret paying your money to watch a movie that was neither pure nor uplifting.

9. Take seriously any sexual problems between you and your spouse.

Many people have terrible marriages and sex lives, thus putting themselves at risk. Monitor your emotions for signs of frustration, stress, depression, and success euphoria. In keeping with the "Elijah syndrome," pastors often fall into sin after their greatest successes, as unbelievable as that might seem. But their guards are down, and they are thus more susceptible to Satan's attacks.

Sexual problems in a marriage are the fault of neither husband nor wife. It is a joint problem that will take a joint commitment to solve. If you have issues in this very personal area of life, sweeping it under the rug and pretending like it doesn't matter will resolve nothing. Bring it to light, talk it through with your spouse, and if you reach an impasse, seek professional help.

10. Limit your late-night television viewing.

Most explicit commercials and shows air after eleven o'clock, and the programming gets raunchier and raunchier as the night progresses. If you are tempted in this area, go to bed when your spouse goes to bed. If you have teenagers in the house who like to stay up late with friends, you are going to have to establish predetermined standards of what they can do and watch after you go to bed. Don't leave them to their own devices.

I recently read about three U.S. soldiers killed in Iraq as they were passing out toys to children. Into the midst of a wonderful scenario of kindness, a suicide bomber intruded and detonated his bomb, killing a number of children as well. What a picture of Satan's attacks! He's not fair, and he comes when we are least expecting him. *We are in a war*, and our lives, our families, and our futures are all on the line every second of every day.

The guidelines discussed in this chapter will serve you well if you learn them and make them second nature. You should never let down your guard and compromise, especially when traveling. I heard about one man who brought his family picture with him on trips and set it on top of the television set in the hotel room. Their beautiful faces reminded him of what was really valuable to him in life.

You are going to make it, child of God. Put some "screens on the windows" and renew your mind in the Word of God. Let integrity guide your decisions, and allow purity to protect your reputation, thus paving the way for another powerful pillar of influence: example.

Questions to Think About

1. How have standards of purity and morality changed even in your lifetime? What things are condoned today that were forbidden in years gone by? How would you answer those, even in the church, who defend alternative lifestyles, divorce, abortion, and other such things?

2. Describe the thought process that leads a person from an immoral thought to an immoral act. How can the train of thought be stopped at any point?

3. If you are single, what standards have you enacted in your life to protect your purity? If you are married, what standards do you and your spouse abide by in order to protect your marriage?

4. How do entertainment choices sometimes lead to moral compromise? Why do you think so many Christians watch the same TV shows and movies as their non-Christian friends and relatives? Should there be a difference between our choices and theirs?

5. What hope is there for someone who has fallen into pornography, adultery, sexual fantasizing, or some other impurity? How can bondages in these areas be broken?

CHAPTER 10

COMMANDMENT 5: EXAMPLE

Let no one look down on your youthfulness, but rather in speech, conduct, love, faith and purity, show yourself—an example of those who believe.

—1 TIMOTHY 4:12

T HE WORD *EXAMPLE* MEANS FOR ONE TO BE "imitated." The Greek word means "to mimic," to behave in such a way that another can copy it exactly. Paul constantly told his disciples, "Be imitators of me" (1 Cor. 4:16; 11:1). Modeling an exemplary lifestyle is the essence of discipleship.

Nothing flawed is mass-produced. When you strive to make yourself an example, you are thus preparing for multiplication. Although only Christ is perfect, you should be able to say, "Follow me as I follow Christ." Your example to your family, your business, and your community makes you a leader. You have a realm of influence, regardless of what you do for a living or what title you bear or don't bear, and in that realm people are watching to see if your actions match your words. Your example is important.

It amazes me to see professional athletes seeking to distance themselves from being role models. They want the influence of their positions but not the pressure of example. Example, however, does not have as much to do with sinful issues as it does with influence.

I remember a coach I had in elementary school. He smoked when he coached us (that's how long ago it was!), and the cigarette bobbed up and down in his mouth as he talked. Years later whenever I told anyone what he had taught me, my lips would purse as I tried to talk the same way he had talked in order to support his cigarette. His example was what was emblazoned in my memory.

I heard once of a British preacher who used to sling his hair as he preached. His inimitable style of preaching was the rave of a certain Bible college. For years following their graduation, all the male students from that Bible college would attempt to sling their hair when they made a powerful point—even some who were bald! In the same vein, many young preachers have tried to imitate Billy Graham to a tee. One young East Texas pastor who had forty members used to look across the handful of farmers in his wood frame church every Sunday and say during his invitation, "Surely, somewhere in this vast concourse of people, there must be one…"

John Donne said, "No man is an island,"[1] and that is particularly true in the body of Christ and the world we mix with. What we do affects others—good or bad—and what they do affects us—good or bad. If we really understood this and began to focus totally on the example we set in the small areas of life, the net product at the end of our lives would be a huge number of people imitating those good qualities. So, here we go with some of the examples we must strive to set.

AN EXAMPLE IN OUR WORK

Order is a key word. God is a God of order, not the author of confusion (1 Cor. 14:33, 40). The children of Israel were a confused, disorganized motley crew when they left Egypt, but when they departed from Sinai, they left with twelve tribes marching in order.

Order precedes multiplication. God never started multiplying plants and animals on the earth until He had first ordered the environment with the proper light, air, and water. Before Jesus fed the five thousand men, He sat them down in groups of fifty. He first brought order out of chaos and then multiplied the fish and bread.

If you pull up to a gasoline pump or an ATM and see a sign hanging on it, that sign probably says "Out of Order." That means you are not going to get a drop of gasoline from that pump or money from the ATM. The lifestyles of far too many Christians are out of order. They thus have nothing to give and no way to multiply their effectiveness for God's kingdom.

Punctuality is one sign of order. When you are constantly late, it speaks of disorganization of your life and time. Some people are late because their closets are so disorganized they can't easily find what they need. They have to frantically paw through the jammed-up hangers looking for that one piece of clothing they want. For others, there is a tendency to oversleep or to procrastinate in getting ready for an event. Still others overcommit to responsibilities and always run behind, trying to get everything done.

When you are late, it conveys a lack of respect for the one you are meeting with. Dr. Cho once told me that if someone is worth meeting with, then that person deserves for me to arrive fifteen minutes early. That's exactly what I did during the six years I met with the governor of Louisiana and his staff.

Each week I left my home an hour early even though it was only a fifteen-minute drive to the Governor's Mansion. I did not want to risk being caught on the interstate in a traffic jam, because you just don't keep a governor waiting! When I arrived at the mansion, I would sit in the parking lot until fifteen minutes before the scheduled meeting time. Then I would go into the meeting room and wait. Often the governor arrived early, and we would have ten minutes alone before anyone else came. What a privilege, but it never would have happened if I had been late.

Being busy is never an excuse for tardiness. In fact, the busier you are, the more essential it is that you manage your time. We all have the same amount of time in a day; it's just that some of us have learned to manage it better than others and, as a result, move through our days in peace and order. The idea of the American rat race that we are all forced to run is a lie.

Jesus never seemed hurried or late. He rose early and moved in a sacred rhythm. Throughout my years in the pastorate, I have sought to set an example of punctuality in our services. I have observed that pastors with lifestyles of tardiness carry this over into their services. This penalizes those who arrive early and forces everyone to wait for those who arrive late.

Many churches have remedied this problem by having their sound man start a countdown clock on their video screens, showing when the service is about to begin. Our leadership at Bethany knows that when the second hand on the clock sweeps across the top of the minute, we are *on*.

I extend this punctuality to all aspects of church ministry. I ask the office staff not to overschedule me so that I stumble late from one appointment to the next. I ask our musicians and technical staff to be present in plenty of time to finish service preparations before people arrive. All around me, I try to create a culture of rest, preparation, and punctuality. All of us will have our interstate challenges from time to time, but we can do our best to make them the exception and not the rule.

Having a strong *work ethic* is another sign of order. Discipline in this area is critical to your example. "The hand of the diligent will rule" (Prov. 12:24), and it is for sure that a lazy, sloppy approach will not. Diligence is rewarded, whether in the home, the workplace, or the church; laziness reaps its own reward.

I think often of my brothers and sisters in the church who are working two jobs, doing shift work, laboring in heavy construction, or doing turnarounds in plants while raising their families, keeping up their homes, and fixing their cars. These hardworking men and women rise early, burn the midnight oil, and fall exhausted into bed each night. They are an example to me, as well as to their neighbors and children.

We must, of course, look at the example of Jesus as He worked. He always rose early: "In the early morning, while it was still dark, Jesus got up, left the house, and went away to a secluded place, and was praying there" (Mark 1:35). His discipline and work ethic were legendary. The disciples could not keep up with Him: "They were on the road going up to Jerusalem, and Jesus was walking on ahead of them; and they were amazed, and those who followed were fearful" (Mark 10:32). Jesus never seemed frazzled by His work, and He never stopped.

I thank the Lord for my father's example of a strong work ethic. From my earliest memories, I remember him involved with all the facets of the church, from construction to conferences. Before joining the staff, one of our first youth pastors arrived in Baton Rouge and pulled onto our property, looking for the church offices. He saw a man on a ladder who was painting the building and asked him, "Excuse me, sir, but can you tell me where the pastor is?" The man replied, "You are looking at him." My father then invited the young man to join him in painting while the two of them talked.

My father started Bethany with no members, so he needed to have an outside job for the first time in his ministry. He worked for five months as a pipe fitter's helper, leaving home each morning at five and catching a ride in front of our home with a carpool of construction workers. He would bring his dress clothes with him to work and change clothes under the Mississippi River bridge during his lunch hour so he could visit people in the hospital. For several years, my mother sold *World Book Encyclopedia* as the fledgling congregation met in our living room and then moved into the first small building. Bethany was born in *work*, and there was no room or time for freeloaders.

Paul had a strong work ethic and set a good example: "I labored even more than all of them, yet not I, but the grace of God with me" (1 Cor. 15:10). He commended those who joined his example: "Greet Mary, who has worked hard for you. . . . Greet

Tryphaena and Tryphosa, workers in the Lord. Greet Persis the beloved, who has worked hard in the Lord" (Rom. 16:6, 12). Somehow, this doesn't quite square with the bankers'-hours mentality of a nine-to-three availability at the office.

Our work should be structured, efficient, and productive. I often ask men who are thinking of starting their own businesses, "Do you have the discipline to be your own boss and require yourself to be at work at eight each morning?" Most admit that they don't and continue in their factory job or whatever other honorable profession they have chosen. To be successful in your profession or God-given calling, you must be a self-starter and have the drive necessary to accomplish what God intended you to accomplish on the earth.

Finally, your *dress* is a sign of order. An unkempt, disheveled appearance is a symptom of a confused lifestyle. I know that casual dress is totally appropriate in today's world, but there is a difference between casual and catastrophic. If you are a man and not a good dresser, let your wife or daughter help you. Let them give you a chart of which pants to wear with which shirt and shoes (or tie if you wear one). If you are a woman, don't become a slave to the latest fashion at the expense of modesty. Get your husband's input or seek the advice of a more mature Christian woman if you are in doubt concerning the appropriateness of a certain article of clothing. You don't have to dress fifty years behind the current style, but always remember the words of Peter: "You should be known for the beauty that comes from within, the unfading beauty of a gentle and quiet spirit, which is so precious to God" (1 Pet. 3:4, NLT).

Like it or not, first impressions do matter. I recall once going into a furniture store with my wife, and the salesman who approached us looked as if he had just crawled out of bed. His shirt was crumpled, his shoes were an unrecognizable color, and his hair looked like someone had slapped him on one side of the head and made all his hair go to the other side! When he turned his back, I motioned to my wife that we needed to move along. That's the effect of dress and appearance.

I hold a weekly business luncheon for business leaders, and I promise you, they are all neatly and appropriately dressed. They know its importance in the business world. When the president of the United States steps up to a microphone, he is dressed in a certain way and carries himself in such a way that the free world feels the power of his authority. He knows his role and dresses the part.

If you were invited to the White House or the Governor's Mansion, not only would you expect the president or governor to be dressed appropriately, but I am sure you would show your respect for those offices by dressing carefully and respectfully. How much more should you show respect to God by the way in which you represent Him in your dress?

The maniac of Gadara, when delivered, was found sitting, clothed properly, and in his right mind. Your life too should be an example of your new life in Christ. When you came to Christ, you became His ambassador and should do all in your power to keep your dress from distracting the lost and disparaging the Savior.

An Example in Your Community

The ever-watching world sees every example you set: the reckless way you drive, your failure to return the grocery cart to the rack in the parking lot, your annoyance with a teller at the bank, or your impatience with a waitress in a restaurant. You may wish you could be anonymous in the community, but it's not possible. There is always someone out there who recognizes you as a pastor or as someone who goes to "that church." Some, because of jealousy or hatred, even look for a reason to denigrate you and prove their point that "all Christians are hypocrites." You should not be paranoid about being under a magnifying glass, but rather look at it as your opportunity to be an example of how Jesus would live in our modern world.

Your *speech* is critical to your example. A cross word, a foul word, or an unkind word will never be forgotten by the person to whom you spoke it. When you are tired and not wanting to be hassled, it is very easy to get loose with your language. But Paul said, "There must be no filthiness and silly talk, or coarse jesting, which are not fitting" (Eph. 5:4). What is the example set by telling an off-color joke? How many times have feelings been hurt by a cut-down or sarcastic remark? How would you feel if the same slur you spoke was spoken about you?

There is no place more important for excellence in speech than in the pulpit. Paul told Timothy to be an example in speech (1 Tim. 4:12) because he knew how easy it is to say something offensive to a congregation. From years of interaction with a congregation, I have learned that certain directions in speaking lead pastors off into the "weeds" and therefore must be avoided. Pastors cannot be so insecure that they sacrifice their good example for the affirmation gained by a laugh from the congregation. Instead, they must carefully consider how each word they say would look printed on the front page of the local newspaper. Would it pass the scrutiny of the community? If not, it doesn't need to be said!

Although education is not essential to godly ministry, neither is ignorance a virtue. We can all be continual students, learning and improving the image we project for Christ. One simple area we can easily incorporate into our example is the use of good grammar and vocabulary. I have been on local television for many years and have often received a note from someone in the community reminding me that a word I used does not exist or that my subject/verb agreement was improper! People are watching. Again, this is not to make you paranoid but to show you the power of your influence and example to others.

An equally important example to maintain is your *courtesy*. Drivers are watching, clerks are watching, policemen are watching. The highway is a stage where you endlessly perform. Blowing your horn at a person stopped at a red light in front of you, bouncing from lane to lane in frustration on the interstate, or wheeling into a parking spot someone else was waiting for can nullify all your lofty words of "Oh, how I love Jesus!"

Nothing aggravates the community more than hearing of a senator, high-profile leader, or minister caught excessively speeding, causing a careless wreck, or showing impatience to one of their constituents or members. Television replays the incident over and over and tries to make it grounds for spiritual impeachment. We all need the grace of God to hold our tempers and to remain calm and controlled in the high-pressure lifestyles we lead.

When tempted to blow your cool, the big question to ask yourself is, is it worth it? Is it worth it to blow your stack to override the return policy of the local department store? Is it worth it to arrive two minutes earlier to your destination? Is it worth it to make a scene in a restaurant over some honey mustard dressing?

Paul's wisdom and example was, "Why not rather be wronged? Why not rather be defrauded?" (1 Cor. 6:7). Go the second mile in your neighborhood and your community. Obey the rules of the highway, supermarket, and bank. Hold back your temper from the high school football referee instead of setting a bad example in front of a stadium full of people. Think in terms of your example to others, not whether you are "right."

An Example in Your Family

You have no greater area of influence than the example of your *family.* Paul spoke often about the exemplary family: "He must be one who manages his own household well, keeping his children under control with all dignity (but if a man does not know how to manage his own household, how will he take care of the church of God?)" (1 Tim. 3:4–5).

Your family is a critical part of your example as a Christian. How you treat your spouse and how you treat and train your children will be replicated by them and observed and judged by others. When your children get into trouble, the world somehow holds you responsible, even if they are adults and gone from your home. (I used to hear about the "terrible twos" but have since discovered they can't compare to the "terrible twenties"!)

Take the example of your family very seriously. Where are your children, and what are they doing? Are they running the parking lots or ransacking the auditorium while you visit with fellow believers after church? Are they rude to their teachers? Are they a constant discipline problem at school?

With six children, Melanie and I have been on the receiving end of teachers, policemen, neighbors, parents, and relatives giving regular updates on the status of our children. We have dealt with serious failures and occasional rebellion in our children. However, despite it all, they are now all serving the Lord with all their hearts. Your family won't be perfect—and it is not expected to be—but because you call yourself a Christian, you do have a standard to uphold before a watching world.

Pastors face an even higher responsibility in their families because, fair or unfair, people look to them for what a Christian family is supposed to be. Being raised in a pastor's home myself, I know the magnifying glass the pastor's family lives under. As a child and young person, I contributed my share of wild ideas and harebrained schemes contrived out of boredom and rebellion. But I made it through all that, and so have many other pastors' kids.

Having an example family, for pastors and laypeople alike, means showing appropriate responses and actions. Again, no one demands perfection, but it is expected, and reasonably so, that you will side with the Word of God when your child must be penalized. When neighbors and teachers see you correctly discipline in love, they respect you for living your faith in a tangible way that aligns with the words you have spoken.

So many Christians fail to realize that their examples have been destroyed because of the lack of discipline in their homes. I cannot count all the times when our children were small that people would come to us outside a restaurant and say, "We have never seen a family so well behaved as yours during that meal. How did you do that?" Watching the total frustration most parents today have when trying to control their little "handfuls" at the table, I understand why so many are in awe when they see polite and well-mannered children. This is order, and it becomes a great example to the watching world.

How you treat your spouse will, of course, be replicated through your children. The memory of a dad who respected his wife by serving her, opening the door for her, addressing her with gentleness, and making her his priority will be forever etched in his children's minds. As my sons marry, I thrill to see how they have treated their wives in the same example. My father's sixty-two years of marriage to my mother has been an incredible example to me of how to grow old together with my wife.

"Brethren, join in following my *example*, and observe those who walk according to the pattern you have in us" (Phil. 3:17, emphasis added). Work on your example, and God will multiply you. Put your life, your emotions, your finances, and your family in order, and watch God enlarge your influence. When you do, God will bring you to work alongside other like-minded people, and you will move into another key pillar in the life of a Christian: relationships.

QUESTIONS TO THINK ABOUT

1. Why is the adage "Do as I say, not as I do" never a valid view for a Christian?

2. Why is a strong work ethic so necessary in your Christian life and ministry? Is there any discrepancy between working hard and trusting God? Discuss. Have you ever known someone who thought that trusting God meant he or she did not need to work or do anything else because "God would provide"? What happened in that situation?

3. What does your dress reveal about you? Do you think there is a certain standard of dress for Christians? If so, what is it, and how do you set those standards? What do you think God thinks about the way we dress?

4. What are some specific ways you can build a good reputation as a Christian in your community? Your workplace? Your family? Your church?

5. Who has the most exemplary family that you have ever known? What makes their family different? What have you learned from them, and how can you incorporate that into your own family?

CHAPTER 11

COMMANDMENT 6: RELATIONSHIPS

Greet Priscilla and Aquila, my fellow workers in Christ Jesus, who risked their own necks for my life.

—ROMANS 16:3–4, NKJV

THE SIXTH GREAT COMMANDMENT OF MINISTRY concerns the importance of relationships. The "rhinestone cowboy" days of Christianity are fading into the sunset. Paul did everything with a team, and in order to be successful, you too are going to have to be able to build and sustain long-term relationships. In today's huge world, the power of networking, kingdom mentality, and accountability will multiply your ability to exert an impact.

Everyone has heard the illustration about the increased productivity of a flock of geese flying in formation. When I look in nature and see the many images of flocks, schools, herds, swarms, colonies, and packs, it becomes obvious that moving together makes sense. In fact, Proverbs itself describes the power of partnership: "The locusts have no king, yet all of them go out in ranks" (Prov. 30:27).

Israel was a ragtag group of individual slaves until Mount Sinai. There they became a powerful, interdependent group of twelve tribes that marched in order and battled in formation. They shifted from an *audience* to an *army* mentality.

Ezekiel saw a valley of dry, disconnected bones (Ezek. 37:1). He walked up and down in them, unsure if they could ever connect. Yet he prophesied over them and watched the bones come together and form muscles and sinews. Then the Lord sent the breath of the Spirit into them, and "they came to life and stood on their feet, an exceedingly great army" (v. 10). Someone once said to me, "God doesn't breathe on anything that isn't connected." God is using small groups, men's and women's networks, pastors' fellowships, denominations, and interdenominational networks to bring relationships together into the *power of one.*

The Power of One

Relationships all stem from God's relationship with Himself in the Trinity: "Let *Us* make man in *Our* image" (Gen. 1:26, emphasis added). The Trinity is a great mystery but can simply be stated as three persons in one essence. The Father, Son, and Holy Spirit form a perfect relationship called "one." Deuteronomy 6:4 expresses it clearly: "Hear, O Israel! The LORD is our God, the LORD is one!"

This perfect relationship between the three persons of the Trinity is heaven's core. When Satan rose up in pride and developed his own agenda, for the first time in eternity there were "two." He was immediately removed from heaven, because around God only the principle of one can operate.

When God made Adam and Eve, He crowned them with heaven's power of one: "For this reason a man shall leave his father and his mother, and be joined to his wife; and they shall become *one* flesh" (Gen. 2:24, emphasis added). Satan was fearful and furious that an earthly relationship had been formed with the same qualities and characteristics as God Himself. He therefore set about to destroy that relationship and succeeded by setting Adam and Eve against each other and later causing one of their sons to kill the other. His agenda throughout the ages has always been to bring confusion and division to powerful relationships.

This power of one is demonstrated throughout the Bible. Solomon's temple was dedicated "when the trumpeters and the singers were to make themselves heard with *one* voice to praise and to glorify the LORD, and when they lifted up their voice accompanied by trumpets and cymbals and instruments of music, and when they praised the LORD saying, 'He indeed is good for His lovingkindness is everlasting,' then the house, the house of the Lord, was filled with a cloud, so that the priests could not stand to minister because of the cloud, for the glory of the LORD filled the house of God" (2 Chron. 5:13–14, emphasis added). Furthermore, David said, "How good and how pleasant it is for brothers to dwell together in unity" (Ps. 133:1).

In the New Testament, Jesus's twelve disciples formed the nucleus of His kingdom. The goal He had in mind for their relationships among themselves was the same as He had with the Father and Holy Spirit: "That they may all be *one*; even as You, Father, are in Me and I in You, that they also may be in Us, so that the world may believe that You sent Me" (John 17:21, emphasis added).

The goal of the Twelve was to become one. On the Day of Pentecost, they were "all with one accord in one place" (Acts 2:1, NKJV), and the same power of God that fell on the temple fell on the church. Paul constantly exhorted the church to be "like-minded, having the same love, being of one accord, of one mind" (Phil. 2:2, NKJV). *This* is the power of one!

THE KINGDOM MENTALITY

My father has often said, "We are not building our own church or denomination—we are building the kingdom." This type of kingdom mentality is the first pillar of healthy relationships among believers and the churches to which they belong. This is perfectly illustrated in Nehemiah's rebuilding of the wall in Jerusalem. He assigned different families and builders to different sections of the wall, but all of them were constructing the same wall. A fault or gap in any section left them all vulnerable.

It's the same way in God's kingdom today. We may each be doing different things, but we are all working on the same wall. Pride and egos involved for "my section" must become secondary to success in the overall project of advancing our Father's kingdom.

The story is told of three men who were laying brick alongside one another. Each was asked, "What are you doing here?" The first said, "Laying brick." The second replied with a little greater perspective and said, "I am building a wall." The third replied with the greatest insight and declared, "I am building the greatest cathedral in all of history." That is kingdom perspective. You can do your little thing, in your little church, with your little group of people, or you can expand your horizons and develop nurturing relationships with other Christians with gifts that complement your own.

Jesus is the King of the kingdom. As its great High Priest, He is building the great temple of God. In every tribe, tongue, people, and nation, He is using committed believers and leaders to build. As long as we share the fundamental core of biblical doctrine, we should be able to work alongside one another as fellow laborers.

The early church did not have various factions, with warring egos and logos. They built together and died together. They lived in the spirit of Benjamin Franklin's words: "We must, indeed, all hang together, or, most assuredly, we shall hang separately."[1]

As I mentioned in an earlier chapter, I meet monthly with about fifteen pastors in our city who are of like mind and have a kingdom mentality. We preach in one another's churches, send offerings for building funds, stand together on moral issues, and target a lost city together. This is possible because those with a kingdom mentality are not insecure.

A pastor once told me that he dared not promote another pastor for fear his own church would not make it. I told him that if his church could not stand, he needed to let it fall. That's what Scripture says: "Unless the LORD builds the house, they labor in vain who build it" (Ps. 127:1, NKJV).

Christians are not in competition with one another, and neither are churches. The success of one is the success of the others, and the failure of one weakens everyone else. We are truly one body—the body of Christ—and we cannot isolate ourselves from one another. When we dig in to protect our perceived territory, nobody wins, and the cause of Christ is hampered.

The need for a kingdom mentality really came front and center in our city during the tragedy of Hurricane Katrina, the worst natural disaster in American history. Tens of thousands of New Orleans residents flooded past our south campus location on Interstate 10 as they escaped the wrath of this monstrous storm. We have three fifteen-story crosses on our property that are visible from the interstate, and hundreds of the evacuees pulled off the highway and stopped at our Center of Hope building adjacent to the crosses.

We took in nine hundred people that night and moved them the next day to our north campus, where we had three auditoriums and gymnasiums to use for shelter. We set up a clinic, showers, school, mailroom, laundry, and cafeteria. We taped off sections of the building for privacy. There was a myriad of details to address.

The needs were so great—and quite frankly, overwhelming—but the body of Christ rose to the challenge. Pastors, church staff, small-group leaders and members, teenagers, children, and people who had never done anything before all united in the face of such tragedy. Some spent long hours cooking, some played with the displaced children, some prayed with the brokenhearted, some were sequestered in offices administrating and organizing the relief effort, and others filled our garners with food, shampoo, soap, and the never-ending list of needed supplies. The body of believers poured themselves out on behalf of the storm's victims and came together in an unprecedented way. We were one, because our mission was one.

After establishing the necessary framework for caring for the evacuees, I called a "town meeting" of these disconnected residents and told them I was acting as their mayor. I told them that we would operate under the law of love and would not tolerate fighting or discord. That second night after the storm, more than seven hundred fifty of the evacuees came forward and gave their hearts to Christ. We never had a single problem with these precious people over our many months of hosting them.

In that first week of the disaster, President Bush and First Lady Laura Bush visited our church for over two hours, and a host of other celebrities and spiritual leaders followed. The crowning beauty of that first week, however, was an impromptu meeting of all area pastors in which two hundred pastors showed up. Most of them, like us, were caring for evacuees in their churches.

The entire world was watching this moment in history. For over four hours, I watched as pastors repented to one another of silly and petty divisions they had tolerated between themselves. Church leaders emerged from that meeting as one. A coordinated effort materialized, and the Pastors Resource Council organization resulted.

In the months that followed, more than seven hundred fifty semi-truckloads of goods arrived from around the world and were distributed to thousands of evacuees in many churches across the city because of a kingdom mentality. The united church became the central driving force of compassion, and this continued until the last evacuee left our church nine months later.

Trust me, when you are dealing with a national crisis, you will develop a kingdom mentality. You realize you cannot possibly meet every need and will duplicate what everyone else is doing unless you work together. Human suffering demands a different mentality.

Our soldiers in Afghanistan and Iraq may not be totally comfortable with all the other nations that fight alongside them, but they rejoice as long as they are shooting in the same direction! So must it be in the church.

Accountability

The second major mind-set needed in relationships is accountability. David and Jonathan formed a covenant of mutual protection and accountability. They exchanged robes, armor, and weapons. Out of love, they voluntarily submitted themselves to each other.

I have that same type of relationship with three men who are over me in the Lord. I have voluntarily given them the right to remove me or discipline me if I default in the areas of doctrine, morals, or finances. They love me in the truest sense and have no ambition to take over my ministry. They are my overseers as well as my peers. They have all been in the pastorate over twenty years and have actively pastored successful, growing churches. Their oversight provides great security for our congregation in the event of my default or accidental death.

Everyone needs accountability in a *real* sense. Real accountability comes when you trust someone to correct and discipline you even if you don't understand or agree with it. It operates on the principle of the "blind side": something you are unable to see, but is nonetheless real and destructive. We all need this, both in our individual lives and in our ministry callings.

I appreciate a "Bridge Out" sign and am not offended by it. It protects me. A bird that is hopping along pecking at a trail of bread crumbs doesn't realize that the trail leads right into a box with a spring to activate a trap. If only someone watching would yell, "Stop!" before it was too late, the bird could escape its imminent doom.

I have watched precious friends of mine follow the "bread crumbs" into the traps of doctrinal error, adultery, and financial impropriety. The feeling of empowerment from the Holy Spirit gives them a sense of invincibility. They curiously study the failings of others while developing no system to correct their own failings before they become "fallings."

Inherent in every system of accountability must be a failsafe trigger that has the power to set down a minister, correct a leader, or confront a believer until all accusations or indiscretions are resolved. The same group that provides accountability should also provide restoration and redirection if necessary. The accountability must have teeth; otherwise, it is only a pretense of discipline. Nothing will change, and the one committing the wrong will be allowed to continue merrily along, much to the detriment of his own soul.

Paul "opposed [Peter] to his face, because he was clearly in the wrong" (Gal. 2:11, NIV). Who in your life has the power to call you to account and challenge unbiblical areas of your life and ministry? Who is watching over your soul "as those who will give an account" (Heb. 13:17)? Most denominations have built-in structures of accountability, but for thousands of churches worldwide, there is no structure for church correction or discipline. True, legitimate accountability, however, will reinvigorate the American church and restore our years of lost credibility before the world.

When I say *accountability*, I mean relationship: gentle, caring, wise, prudent counsel. Paul said that only those who are spiritual should deal with those overtaken in a fault (Gal.

6:1). However, I also believe that the accountability must be real so that the one being corrected cannot just cut off the one who confronts his character.

"Iron sharpens iron, so one man sharpens another" (Prov. 27:17), and where I am from, that means the sparks fly! The world has watched as exposed ministers are "restored" after a few weeks of sideline rest. They know that this does not measure up to any real standard of accountability. It is actually the most merciful thing in the world to give a fallen minister a long period of time to be rehabilitated in his marriage, finances, training, and reputation. As in any rehab, allowing someone with a life-controlling problem to go back into the same environment prematurely only perpetuates the problem.

Boundaries empower. An athlete running the football down the field feels secure within the boundaries. A citizen going the speed limit with proper registration of his car has nothing to fear from police officers. In the section on purity, we saw the importance of boundaries of accountability in marriage.

In doctrine, I respect my boundaries and always bring any new revelation or emphasis to those in spiritual authority over me to test its long-term validity before placing it before a trusting congregation. The same holds true for any small-group leader or person involved in any type of church ministry. No matter how powerful the "revelation" received in private prayer, it must be submitted to proper authority.

In finances, I follow the accounting rules for nonprofit organizations and do not refute my accounting department if something I am doing is in the gray area. They are there for my protection and empowerment.

David said, "Let the righteous smite me in kindness and

reprove me; it is oil upon the head; do not let my head refuse it" (Ps. 141:5). Accountability, evidently, brings a greater anointing (oil) upon your head!

NETWORKING: THE POWER OF A TEAM

The last important advantage of relationships is that it multiplies your efforts through networking and team management. We know that "two are better than one, because they have a good reward for their labor....And a threefold cord is not quickly broken" (Eccles. 4:9, 12, NKJV). Jesus used the power of a team as described in the legendary book *The Master Plan of Evangelism* by Dr. Robert Coleman. In this book, Dr. Coleman demonstrates the eight steps of forming a team and highlights how the twelve men on Jesus's team multiplied Christ's ministry worldwide.[2]

I have followed this plan to develop missions worldwide (as described in chapter 3). With this strategy in place, the power of teamwork is rapidly bringing the gospel to unreached areas. One Liberian pastor took four thousand dollars and bought a cassava farm. He then used the proceeds of the crop to send out 300 new church planters to unreached people groups. One year later, 289 of the church planters had successfully planted a church, and there were 20,000 new believers in those churches!

At the writing of this book, another pastor from Sierra Leone has received thirty thousand dollars to buy two hundred bicycles to provide transportation for pastors in training. By gaining mobility, his two hundred pastoral candidates are planting five churches, for a total of a thousand village churches. What a tremendous investment!

Relationships are the building blocks for teams, and teams

build networks. Networks form a "net" that can harvest millions of souls. Therefore, *relationships* are the most important thing in the gospel. A church will be only as successful as is its team—period. And the effectiveness of each team member exponentially increases when they are in life-giving relationships with one another.

Here at Bethany, our men's and women's teams do some really amazing, creative things together. One women's team put together an entire day outreach to a large group of at-risk girls. They named their event "Prada Girl" (from "prodigal") and did skits, workshops, and small-group discussions on purity. So successful was the event that at the end of the day, many girls wept and testified of their intent and desire to walk in sexual purity. That is but one testimony of what a committed, God-centered team can accomplish.

College teams recruit players with speed, and suddenly they are in the national title chase. It's the same for any church. Thriving churches that influence their communities recruit teams of committed, loyal powerhouse leaders, as the apostle Paul did. He traveled in a team with Luke (his doctor) and a representative from most of the churches he had planted. He mentored them and then let them represent him: "I trust in the Lord Jesus to send Timothy.... For I have no one like-minded, who will sincerely care for your state" (Phil. 2:19–20, NKJV).

Here are some things that effective teams have in place:

1. Written expectations (everyone knowing his or her role)
2. Loyalty (no separate agendas)

3. Communication (constant flow of
   information)
4. Empowerment (not possessiveness,
   manipulation, or control)

Relationships determine your overall kingdom impact. Long-term, faithful relationships reveal consistency in marriage and ministry. As with Christ's apostles, relationships disciple and multiply.

Paul's MO (method of operation) was clear and easy to duplicate. Pastors too must lay out values that multiply, both within their churches and cross-culturally, and believers must eagerly embrace these values. We call these values your philosophy, and that is the next commandment of ministry.

Questions to Think About

1. Since Jesus was God, why do you think He still chose a team to work with? Why is it dangerous to be a lone ranger in your Christian walk or ministry?

2. You have many types of relationships in your life. List them in order of priority, and think about how each area enhances your relationship with God and others.

3. Think about a time when you tried to do something for God all on your own and another time when you accomplished something for the kingdom as part of a team. Which way was more effective? Why?

4. Where do the boundaries lie concerning our accountability to others and their accountability to us? What happens if we take the stance that we are accountable to no one but God? What happens if we feel that every decision we make must be approved by someone "over" us?

5. What has been the most effective team you have ever been a part of? What made it so successful, and what did you learn from being a part of it?

Chapter 12

Commandment 7: Philosophy

For our boasting is this: the testimony of our conscience that we conducted ourselves in the world in *simplicity* and godly *sincerity,* not with fleshly wisdom but by the grace of God, and more abundantly toward you.

—2 Corinthians 1:12, NKJV, emphasis added

Philosophy strikes the image of mental giants stroking their beards. A philosophy, however, is simply a system of givens. It is a framework in which you make judgments and decisions. When you have a life or ministry philosophy, decision making becomes easy for you and everyone else associated with you.

The *Oxford American Dictionary* defines philosophy as "a theory or attitude held by a person or organization that acts as a guiding principle for behavior." Is your view of church flashy or functional? Is it local oriented or missions oriented? Is it geared toward the wealthy or the needy? Is it generous or stingy? A church's philosophy of ministry guides the personality of that church and its ministry as well as the members who participate in it. So if you are a pastor, you are going to have to develop a philosophy of ministry that clearly articulates what you believe and why. If you are a church member, you too will need to think through your philosophy concerning church and find a local body that best exemplifies it. When like-minded pastors and members join forces, explosive power is unleashed to advance God's kingdom.

A church's philosophy usually originates with the church planter, the apostolic person who laid the foundation of the church. My father laid the foundation for our church in 1963, and we have maintained that philosophy for over four decades. If something comes along that is popular but does not fit our philosophy, we say, "It's just not Bethany." It is critical that a church's philosophy be formulated and communicated. Everyone coming in should know what that particular church's ministry schema is and how it makes them unique.

The apostle Paul had a philosophy of ministry that represented his values and structure. In the verse at the beginning of this chapter, Paul's philosophy shines through in the words *simplicity* and *godly sincerity*. Let's look at how Paul thought of ministry and seek to develop something similar.

SIMPLICITY

Genius is the ability to make something simple from something complex. The Greek word for *simple* implies a narrow focus, a single mind. Having raised six children, I know that kids are masters at making things complex. If they enter a room with a closet full of toys, they will take every toy out and play with all of them until the floor is totally cluttered. It is certainly not a mark of maturity to see how complex you can make your environment.

In the church world, we often feel we are being productive if we are spinning new programs and ministries on a daily basis. And sometimes our members also equate activity with spirituality. So we add programs, which adds staff, which adds offices, which adds buildings, which adds finances, which adds pressures. But everyone knows that when you scatter your shot, you really can't do much damage.

Think of the difference between a beach ball and a bowling ball to illustrate this point. A beach ball is big, fluffy, and fun, but it can't do any damage. A bowling ball, however, can knock down a door. That's what you have to have in a church: concentrated, consolidated effort with the power to achieve goals, not just the latest and greatest ministry fad that comes along.

"Bigger is better" is not necessarily true, as many worn-out senior pastors and harried church members will testify. Their lives have become complex mazes of budgets, departments, committee meetings, building programs, properties, organizations, and publicity. The simple power of the local church is left far behind as these well-intentioned though misguided pastors charge forward (with "Master Charge," that is!). And in their wake follow the tired, flustered believers who try to keep up with them and emulate their pattern of "working for the Lord."

But Jesus said, "My yoke is easy and My burden is light" (Matt. 11:30). Whatever happened to the rest Jesus promised in that passage? With complexity has come stress, and with stress has come sin.

The late John Osteen, who was a good friend of my father,

had a dream in which the Lord appeared to him and showed him a cross. The Lord instructed him to pick up the cross. He leaned down and prepared to shoulder the great weight, but when he lifted it, he realized it was made of Styrofoam!

Through this dream, the Lord redirected him from assembling a huge office and staff for an international ministry and instead showed him how to streamline and simplify. His church, now pastored by his son Joel, has continued this philosophy and has become the largest church in America. The Osteens' simple, people-oriented philosophy of excellence has struck a national chord and endeared them to millions.

Simple is "sticky." That's what advertising gurus have discovered. In the book *Made to Stick* by Chip and Dan Heath, simplicity is extolled as the element that makes complex ideas stick. The authors refer to such well-known slogans as "It's the economy, stupid," "The real thing," and "Just do it" as classic examples of simple ideas that have stuck. They offer this equation to help explain it: simple = core + compact.[1] In other words, keeping things simple is the result of taking one core idea and expressing it in a compact form.

In organization, simplification saves money and cuts through red tape and bureaucracy. "Keep it simple, stupid" (KISS) means that the simpler a concept, the easier it is to implement at the grassroots level. That is why entire organizations spend days boiling down their visions and mission statements to something simple and transferable.

We have only a certain amount of focus ability. I have read that a lion in a cage gets confused by the four legs of the stool his trainer holds before him and simply sits paralyzed because he can't focus. The same thing happens to you when too many things demand your attention. So, pastors, *simplify* your ministry budgets, positions, and programs. Find a guiding philosophical question you can apply to determine if they are still relevant. A good one might be, does it win souls and make disciples? Or, does it teach the Scriptures? Or, does it build strong families? Believers too should ask themselves these pointed questions about their churches' ministries and the ones they become involved in.

Much of our problem with complexity stems from a keeping-up-with-the-Joneses mentality in ministry. Pastors hear of another local church in the city that has a ministry to redheads over twenty-nine but under thirty-one and immediately open such a ministry themselves! They learn that a bus ministry in another church is really making an impact, so they decide they need a bus ministry too. What they don't know, however, is that the other church is in the process of phasing out and selling all their buses! Or, worst of all, they visit a conference in a neighboring state and come home with an armload of materials for the same weary, worn-out core who has followed them through three other directions.

It's not just pastors who are prone to complicating ministry. Good, God-fearing believers do it too. Maybe because they genuinely want to serve God and expand His kingdom, they find themselves involved in anything and everything without evaluating its rightful place in their lives at that time. Sadly, some have neglected family duties, shirked work responsibilities, and abandoned simple daily pleasures as their lives became increasingly complex and demanding—all in the name of the Lord.

I recall one family in our church whose complicated lifestyle led to a financial crisis. They came to us for help, and we began the process. We first listed all their debt, and unbelievably, it came to over one page of single-spaced items! Their complex lifestyle and illogical management of their money had their marriage, family, health, and minds in a convoluted swirl of confusion. We worked with them, and by simplifying and prioritizing, they were able to get completely out of debt in less than three years. But it couldn't have happened without their willingness to reexamine their life and simplify it. Complex, confused choices always bring major conflict, crisis, and chaos.

Simple is better. I always ask myself this simple question about anything we are doing: *Is this simplifying our ministry or piling more on top of our already strained resources and workforce?* Our federal government is a prime example of what happens when an organization gets bogged down with regulations and programs that often conflict and compete with one another. Staff meetings then become budget battles as department heads compete for limited resources.

The same can happen in the church. I like to say that the average pastor is under such stress that he resembles a longtailed cat in a room full of rocking chairs! The only solution is to downsize, consolidate, simplify, and rest. The early apostles knew this. That's why they delegated many responsibilities to others so they could devote themselves to prayer and the ministry of the Word (Acts 6:4).

One of our missionary partners in Mexico was becoming frazzled by all the time he had to spend raising financial support for other missionary couples. The Lord instructed him to go on about his work and let those who could not thrive go home. Sometimes you have to step back, trust God, and let the chips fall where they may.

I close this section on simplicity with an illustration from the old Ed Sullivan show from the 1960s. Ed often had as a guest a man whose talent was spinning plates. The man would begin his act by spinning one plate and placing it on top of a stick. As he set the stick down (with the plate still spinning on top), he started another plate spinning. He continued until he was spinning many plates, but he had to keep running back to keep the first plates going. Without his personal attention, each plate would eventually wobble and fall.

Isn't that a perfect description of so many pastors and Christians? We have spawned so many ideas and projects that require our personal momentum to sustain. But hear me clearly: If the Holy Spirit does not sustain them, *let them fall.* Simplify your life and ministry for the long haul. Your health will improve, your marriage will last, and your joy in serving God will return.

Sincerity

A second important aspect of ministry philosophy is *sincerity.* You may have heard that this word comes from the Latin words *sine cere,* meaning "without wax." In ancient days, pottery merchants sold pots with that marking to differentiate them from cheaper pots that had cracked and been repaired with wax and paint. It came to imply something that was real, transparent, and genuine.

The apostle Paul was real. He said, "For our proud confidence is this: the testimony of our conscience, that in holiness and godly sincerity, not in fleshly wisdom but in the grace of

God, we have conducted ourselves in the world, and especially toward you" (2 Cor. 1:12). Sincerity, therefore, is keeping your conscience clean before the world.

He continued, "For we are not like many, peddling the word of God, but as from sincerity, but as from God, we speak in Christ in the sight of God" (2 Cor. 2:17). Religious panhandling and hucksterism were obviously around even in Paul's day.

"Keeping it real" has become the watchword of reality television. However, in the church, we tend to drift into methods, attitudes, and atmospheres that appear insincere and unreal. When new people enter a church, within a couple of minutes they mentally rate the "sincerity index" on a scale from one to ten. If they sense genuineness and transparency, they remain interested. If they conclude that the emotions are hype or not genuine, they can't wait to leave.

The spin doctors from Washington and Hollywood are infamous for their ability to present whatever picture they want of a situation. Like a cat falling from a roof, they always land on their feet. They can doctor any situation that portrays them in a bad light into something positive or unimportant. These obvious cover-ups offend smart, sensible people. Because of this pervasive lack of reality, our younger generation grows increasingly cynical about both the church and government.

I have often been able to help believers through financial crises just by urging them to be sincere with their creditors. Though their natural tendency is to avoid those they are having trouble paying, I counsel them to call their creditors and let them know the exact situation. I tell them to be completely forthright, not spinning, bending, or flavoring the story in any way. To their surprise, creditors are more confident of a person's credit risk and thus more willing to work with him when they perceive he is being truthful. It's another story, however, when they hear "honest Otto, the used car salesman," on the other end of the line.

My mother, in the early days of Bethany, used to collect delinquent encyclopedia sales accounts. One day she knocked on the door of a house, and a little girl answered. Very innocently, the child said, "My mother said to tell you she's not home!" That, of course, is not sincerity, but often the route too many choose. Make a decision to be truthful and sincere, regardless of the outcome; and God will honor you for it.

I have been doing a network television program for twenty years. It is ninety seconds long and runs at 6:50 a.m. on the two major networks in our city. Beginning that program in a time when major ministry scandals were hitting the evening news did not help me. However, the Lord impressed me that sincerity would open the door to hearts. As I tape that simple program, I focus each day on being exactly who I am to one other person watching me. It has taken skeptics and cynics aback. They watch me day after day for years, eventually dropping their defenses and receiving the simple Word of God. The door to minister for six years at the Governor's Mansion, which I mentioned earlier, came as a result of that little program.

Why do we so often feel we have to project an image of someone we are not? The world is desperate for Jesus but has a hard time finding a messenger who is sincere. At Bethany, we do not allow anything in our church that is fake or projects a lie. By transparently opening our hearts, we build confidence and stability in the church and before the world.

When you date a person who is insincere, your "discerner"

goes off and tells you it is time to move on. The same holds true for any aspect of your life as a Christian. Run every major decision you have to make through the "sincerity grid" before you move forward. Stay true to who you are and your philosophy in life. The result will be a genuine, open, healthy life that draws people to you and the God you represent.

SACRIFICE

The last philosophical pillar on which we rest our ministry is *sacrifice.* When I read of all the apostle Paul went through in his ministry (2 Cor. 11:23–27), I feel privileged to do ministry in America. Though I have never suffered like Paul, I do remember my missionary days in Africa when Melanie and I had no electricity or running water for as long as six months at a time. That area of the Nigerian delta region was so primitive that we spent most of our time simply surviving. We spent sweltering nights behind closed windows to escape the biting gnats. In trying to cope, we soaked the sheets through with perspiration, but there was no alternative. Taking cold baths, depending on a kerosene refrigerator that made an ice cube every few days, boiling and filtering water multiple times before drinking, and constantly fighting malaria became our way of life.

When I returned from those two years on the field, I possessed an appreciation for missionaries and their struggles. As I walked into an American grocery store full of thousands of brands of thousands of items, I recalled that in a store in the national capital of one African nation, there had been one item available in the entire store: pineapple marmalade! Additionally, all toilet paper was exported to other countries, and people stood in lines for little cans of milk. Despite all the lack, however, some of the national pastors, who received fifty dollars a month for support, had incredible ministries.

I once heard a pastor say, "If there is not a Hilton, I am not a missionary." I thought to myself of the time when we traveled to a remote village in a small canoe with an outboard motor. The national workers kept swatting the dangerous tsetse flies that kept landing on us. As the hours passed, it began to feel like I was sitting on a broom handle, so narrow was the makeshift seat in the canoe. Finally, by nightfall, we approached the village.

Peering into the darkness, I could see kerosene lanterns on the shore. As we drew closer, I soon realized there were hundreds of waiting people. They whisked us from our small boat and ushered us to the center of town, demanding that we preach then and there! Those four hundred villagers had waited the entire day, staying home from their fields, because they had heard we were coming. With only a short message preached from a small mound of dirt in the center of the village, virtually the entire population gave their hearts to the Lord.

No, there wasn't a Hilton there in that African village. There wasn't much of anything—only a group of isolated, hard-to-reach people, hungry for the gospel and willing to sacrifice to hear it.

Of course, I do believe that the gospel message on tithing and giving will transform people's finances from a curse to a blessing. I have seen poor Haitians become prosperous by their country's standards simply by learning to tithe their income. I also believe that God wants His people to be blessed. Paul said, "My God will supply all your needs according to His riches in glory in Christ Jesus" (Phil. 4:19).

Paul further stated, "The elders who rule well are to be considered worthy of double honor, especially those who work hard at preaching and teaching. For the Scripture says, 'You shall not muzzle the ox while he is threshing,' and 'The laborer is worthy of his wages'" (1 Tim. 5:17–18). I believe pastors and ministry workers should be well paid so that they don't have to spend their time conjuring up all kinds of financial schemes to make ends meet. There is an acceptable median of support for spiritual leaders that enables them to walk comfortably with any level of society without appearing excessive. Believers too have a right to use their hard-earned income to meet the needs of their families. However, when we lose touch with the necessity of sacrifice so that others may hear the gospel, we depart from a key philosophy of our faith.

The key of any biblical truth, including finances, is balance. Without finances, Christians can do nothing for others worldwide. It has been my joy on several occasions to channel up to a million dollars to a missions project or outreach. But if I begin to think of myself as a worthy recipient of those blessings, I depart from Paul's philosophy. Never forget: you are blessed to be a blessing.

At Bethany, we have endeavored through the years to give 25 percent of our annual income to local and foreign missions outreaches. There are many other things we could do with that income, but it is part of our philosophy that sacrificial missions fulfills the heart of Jesus in the Great Commission. Those who call our church "home" know that missions is a top priority, and because they have embraced the philosophy of sacrificial giving, we have been able to do far more than we ever dreamed possible.

When considering a particular expenditure, a good guiding test for any church or individual believer is to ask these questions: Could we do without this thing and instead use those funds to plant churches worldwide? Are we moving beyond meeting our needs and instead becoming self-focused? Paul seemed to have a happy, balanced ministry without accumulating many earthly possessions, so we know that it is possible. It's just not a popular message that self-indulgent people in affluent societies like to hear.

Keep it simple, keep it sincere, and *keep it sacrificial.* Perhaps your philosophy will include these phrases or other similar expressions that are the foundation for your decision making. Sit down and examine yourself to be sure that you have not departed from the foundation laid for you. If the foundation from the past is flawed, make a shift. Pastors, communicate with your staff and congregation the new values you hold dear, and then together write them on your hearts. Values translate into actions, from the sanctuary to the church offices to the church checkbook! Believers, be open to having your philosophy of ministry challenged and expanded and your horizons enlarged beyond your present limitations.

These first seven commandments will lay a strong foundation in anyone's life and ministry. Though not glamorous, a strong foundation is necessary, but once you have it in place, you are ready to move to the construction phase. The last three commandments of ministry will construct the building that everyone will see, and the first of these commandments is faith.

QUESTIONS TO THINK ABOUT

1. What is your philosophy of life, and how did you develop it? How has it guided you in difficult situations? What is your philosophy of ministry, and how did you develop it? How has it guided you in difficult situations?

2. Since coming to Christ, has your Christian walk become simpler or more complex? Why do Christians sometimes seem to drift from their first simple joy of knowing Christ? What can you do if you have departed from this position?

3. Why is sincerity such a crucial ingredient in our witness to the lost? What characteristics are they looking for in Christians to prove their sincerity?

4. Sacrifice is almost a lost word among some groups of Christians. What has caused the church to lose sight of this foundational truth? How does the belief that God wants to bless us fit with the belief that the Christian walk demands sacrifice?

5. Examine yourself: Does the church you belong to have a guiding philosophy that you can articulate? Have you embraced this philosophy as your own? In which area do you most need to see personal change: simplicity, sincerity, or sacrifice? What could you begin doing to make these values part of your daily life?

CHAPTER 13

COMMANDMENT 8: FAITH

> After these things the word of the LORD came
> to Abram in a vision, saying, "Do not fear,
> Abram, I am a shield to you; your reward shall
> be very great."
>
> —GENESIS 15:1

THERE IS A NATURAL WORLD, AND THERE IS A SPIRI-
tual world. The spiritual world is more real than the
natural because the natural sprang from the spiritual.
Some call the spirit world the "fourth dimension," meaning
that it is above the natural space/time realities of lines, planes,
and cubes. Faith is what brings you into this dimension that
the apostle Paul called "heavenly places."

Walking in the fourth dimension is like walking with your
head above the clouds. In the first three dimensions of the
natural world are your circumstances, but in the fourth dimension, the dimension of faith, is the victory of Christ in His
resurrection and ascension. When Peter walked on water, he
was moving in the spirit world and in the fourth dimension;
only when fear entered his heart did he sink into the natural
world of his circumstances.

The Scripture verse at the beginning of this chapter is part of a story about the spirit world. God's first words to Abram in this vision were, "Do not fear." Faith and fear cannot coexist. Doubt, fear, and unbelief can stop any miracle. Jesus knew this and often had to remove people from unbelieving villages in order to get them healed (Mark 8:22–23).

Faith is a critical factor for success in the Christian life. If you become defeated, negative, skeptical, and fearful, your spiritual boat cannot float; and like Peter, you'll be in danger of sinking. In this chapter, I will attempt to build your faith to the level of conquest.

FAITH AND VISION

Let's go back to our verse in Genesis 15:1. Here in this verse is the first mention of the word *vision* in the Bible (the clearest teaching on a subject is the first mention in the Bible). God appeared to Abram in a vision, giving him a glimpse into the spirit world. Vision is similar to someone's pulling back a curtain, giving you a glimpse of an object, and then letting the curtain fall back into place. It is a snapshot of the eternal. The shutter opens and a picture is taken, but the development of the image takes time. *All faith begins with a vision.* You must see what God sees in the spirit world, and then your faith will rise above your circumstances.

Your vision as a Christian, whether in a pastoral capacity or on a personal level, is critical. In Genesis 15:5, God drew Abram from his tent and brought him outside to look up into the night sky. There He spoke to him of a vision greater than Abram could have imagined. Like Abram, many Christians have a tent mentality in vision, a limited, natural, confined vision. All they can see is something that is struggling to survive.

Your vision is like car headlights: you are either on low beam or high beam. If you're driving on low beam, you are afraid to move past your vision, so you slow down. But when you're driving on high beam, your vision expands and you move faster. More vision, more motion is the way it works.

"Do you see anything?" Jesus asked the blind man (Mark 8:23). Because the man initially experienced only partially healed vision, he saw "men…like trees, walking around" (v. 24). I know a lot of people like that: they struggle to see a clear vision of their future, their personal growth, and their effectiveness for God's kingdom.

The size of your vision is often determined by your office or position. An apostle sees the entire world, a prophet sees the nation, an evangelist sees a city, a pastor sees a church, and a teacher sees his disciples. Businessmen see their companies, schoolteachers see their students, and parents see their children. The size of your vision determines your measure of faith, and God alone can increase your vision. However, once you know your office or position, your faith begins to stretch to fill your vision.

Years ago, I had a Stretch Armstrong doll whose rubberized arms could stretch to a width of six feet. Holding him up in front of the church, I would pull his arms wide as I encouraged everyone, "Str…e…e…e…tch your faith!" They visually got the point of fulfilling the measure of their faith.

God then took Abram outside (Gen. 15:5) and told him to lift up his eyes and see the stars. God told him that each star was a future child or descendant. In those countless stars were the faces of Abram's posterity. Like Abram, we need to move outside our tents, look up, and see what does not yet exist in the natural.

I often ask the Lord to show me His vision for my future because *vision activates faith.* Vision becomes the blueprint for the future. Both Moses and David received visions, one for building the tabernacle and the other for building the temple. Both saw that vision in the Spirit and then wrote down the plans, which eventually came to pass.

Plans produce buildings, if they are written down and specific. That is why you *must* write your vision down and keep it before your eyes: "Then the LORD answered me and said, 'Record the vision and inscribe it on tablets, that the one who reads it may run. For the vision is yet for the appointed time; it hastens toward the goal and it will not fail. Though it tarries, wait for it; for it will certainly come, it will not delay'" (Hab. 2:2–3).

FAITH AND TRUST

Concerning Abram, Genesis 15:6 says, "Then he believed in the LORD; and He reckoned it to him as righteousness." The word translated "believed" in Hebrew is *awman*, the root word for "amen." It is the same word used to depict a nurse, or mother, holding a baby. Like me, you have probably held your infant children in your arms and felt the dead weight of a totally relaxed and sleeping child. The baby lies, totally relaxed in your arms, fully trusting in your ability to care and provide for him.

This same picture applies to faith. It speaks of a state of being, a relaxed posture of rest. It is not struggling and straining. It is a faith that lies in complete trust. As David said, "Surely I have composed and quieted my soul; like a weaned child rests against his mother, my soul is like a weaned child within me" (Ps. 131:2).

Abram accepted the vision of millions of children and simply said amen! For many, however, faith is not that simple. For them, it's like struggling to learn the fundamentals of a golf swing. If you think about every muscle, angle, and speed while you are swinging, every one of your shots will be terrible. But if you relax and trust your muscle memory (without too much thinking), you will almost always hit the ball.

I hear some teach on faith and it reminds me of that golf swing: *Hold on...turn loose...think this...say that.* I get tired just listening to all the instructions! But, really, faith is more about *receiving* than *doing.* Paul told the Hebrew believers, "We who have believed enter that rest" (Heb. 4:3). And Jesus told blind Bartimaeus, "Receive your sight" (Luke 18:42). The problem was not with Jesus's love or will but with Bartimaeus's receiving.

I believe *rest* is a huge issue with ministers, Christian leaders, and ordinary believers. They all struggle and strive to "make it happen." They have no rest or peace because of a lack of trusting in God to bring it to pass. Their families break up, they make impetuous decisions, and their health disintegrates because of a lack of rest. They stop laughing and start taking themselves far too seriously. Their faces are contorted with anxiety over the latest drama in the choir, board meeting, and office. In the small group, they fixate over the number coming to their meetings. In the home, they wonder why everyone else seems to get the blessings that escape them. Each one is on a never-ending merry-go-round of self-help and good works to attain what God has promised to freely give.

To all of you who are reading this book, I have a word from the Lord: *relax!* My major professor in college helped me understand this principle when he defined the term *abide* in John 15 as "working to full capacity in a relaxed state of faith." I have learned the same thing from my father. His favorite phrase about ministry is, *Hang loose…keep it simple…travel light!* After spending many years under the grind of ministry pressure, he decided to work *with* God instead of *for* God. That is what makes all the difference.

Faith relaxes in the vision you have seen and turns the timetable over to God. After all, a promise is a promise. When a child hears a promise from a parent, the child *should* relax and rest on the word of the parent. But when we, God's children, don't see the vision come to pass, we tend to panic, as Abram did.

It took Abram twenty-four years after receiving his vision before his trust turned to sight. He should have just waited for the promise to manifest and not panicked, but instead he took matters into his own hands, and Ishmael resulted. Perhaps you have waited so long you are ready to *do something.* That will not bring your vision to pass; it will only delay it. Remember, the longer you patiently stand in faith, the greater glory it will bring to God when it comes. Say, "Amen!"

FAITH AND WORDS

Much has been said in recent years about our words and their effect on our faith. Proverbs does say, "Death and life are in the power of the tongue" (Prov. 18:21). And in the New Testament, James tells us that the tongue is like a ship's rudder

(James 3:4–5). We should not become paranoid about our words, but at the same time, we should be careful to choose words that bring life. Words are powerful rudders that guide our lives and ministries.

Your words must come into agreement with the vision God has given you. You can negate your vision by constantly speaking words of fear, strife, and unbelief. Jesus tied your faith to your words: "Truly I say to you, whoever says to this mountain, 'Be taken up and cast into the sea,' and does not doubt in his heart, but believes that what he says is going to happen, it will be granted him" (Mark 11:23).

As a pastor, I have realized that praise is the language of faith. Abraham "did not waver in unbelief but grew strong in faith, *giving glory to God*" (Rom. 4:20, emphasis added). When I doubt and become pessimistic, my words change from thanksgiving to grumbling. Such negative mentality and conversation cloud my vision, drop me back down into the natural world, and influence those around me to lose hope.

Nehemiah understood the power of negative words when the men of Judah, out of fear and discouragement, said, "The strength of the burden bearers is failing, yet there is much rubbish; and we ourselves are unable to rebuild the wall" (Neh. 4:10). He replied, "Do not be afraid of them; remember the Lord who is great and awesome, and fight for your brothers, your sons, your daughters, your wives and your houses" (v. 14).

The greatest example of the power of words to cancel vision is the familiar story of the twelve men who spied out the Promised Land. The contrast between a good report and an evil report is seen right here: "Then Caleb quieted the people before Moses and said, 'We should by all means go up and take possession of it, for we will surely overcome it.' But the men who had gone up with him said, 'We are *not able* to go up against the people, for they are too strong for us'" (Num. 13:30–31, emphasis added).

God told those ten spies who had negatively influenced the people that "just as you have spoken in My hearing, so I will surely do to you" (Num. 14:28). There is the serious connection between your words and your faith! The ten spies with the evil report died in the desert, but Joshua and Caleb, the two spies who spoke a good report, journeyed into the land of vision.

Watch your conversation and the words of those around you. We know that reality demands us to converse about things, but we should always dwell on, speak about, and praise with the language of faith. *Failure to live by this principle has trapped many believers in discouragement and defeat.* As you are reading this chapter, repent of any negative words of unbelief that have set your course, and begin to praise the Lord every day for His promises of growth, increase, and blessing.

FAITH AND GROWTH

In speaking to the Corinthians, Paul reminded the early church that "God was causing the growth" (1 Cor. 3:6). God wants you to grow in your walk with Him, and He wants churches to grow as they follow Him. Faith begins with vision, continues with your words, and ends with growth. In the Book of Acts, the church grew, first by addition and then by multiplication. No pastor should feel condemned or belittled by the size of his growth because many factors control that: the size of the city, the spiritual labor that preceded him, and the level of his spiritual gifting. However, when many pastors hear reports of huge church growth, it has a negative, discouraging impact upon them because they compare their size and increase with other national examples.

The same thing happens on a smaller scale when small-group leaders compare themselves with one another or the local women's ministry is compared to one of national scope and influence. Such comparisons are not only unfair, but they also quench faith.

Paul gave us the key to growth in the first part of the above Scripture: "I planted, Apollos watered, but God was causing the growth." The vision of growth, regardless of the venue, is not about planting "weeds," which spring up quickly, but planting "trees," which require years of growth. And the best long-range plan for healthy growth is discipleship; that is, growing people. We must grow people, who will in turn grow other people, who will in turn grow the church, which in turn expands God's kingdom. This means everyone—from pastor to ministry leader to small child—has a vital part to play in seeing the church grow.

Ingenious pastors have come up with rallies, campaigns, events, and marketing ideas to grow the church, but when the push is over, the church goes back to its original size. There is no lasting fruit. True growth, however, comes only from growing people.

David discipled his band of four hundred men who were "in distress . . . in debt, and . . . discontented . . . and he became captain over them" (1 Sam. 22:2). They became his mighty men, and thousands of other soldiers joined their ranks. There's a lesson for pastors and ministry leaders to learn from this: Develop the core. Work with the faithful. Believe in people and develop them. Don't rush to growth, but patiently believe in them.

My son Joel has developed one of the largest youth ministries in America by this principle. He and his late wife worked for several years developing a band of faithful leaders, dealing with all the warts of their character. These leaders did the same with others. Suddenly, growth began. From seven hundred fifty youth in August of 2005, their groups grew to over six thousand youth by December of 2007. This J-curve approach seems slower at first, but it eventually results in growth through radical prayer, radical evangelism, and radical discipleship. Faith is critical to this powerful paradigm and involves all the concepts I have taught in this chapter.

One of the young men in our youth ministry illustrates perfectly what unleashed faith can do. Coming from a family with a very dysfunctional father, this young man struggled with low self-esteem and lack of vision. My son Joel, however, saw something in him and personally discipled him in his character and helped him stretch his faith. The effects were staggering. As his faith in God grew, this young man, who already led a small group, began to multiply and quickly developed a team of leaders. Soon God gave him a beautiful young wife of faith, and the two of them currently minister to more than one thousand youth in the groups that they oversee!

The early disciples, such as Barnabas, were "full of the Holy Spirit and of faith. And considerable numbers were brought to the Lord" (Acts 11:24). It can be the same for you too. Begin to release your faith for growth, harvest, and increase. What's stopping you from reaching your community in a tangible way? Who says you can't have a group of women in your home for coffee and the Word once a week? Why not turn that unfinished room into a gathering place of fun and ministry for your teenagers and their friends? You have only one lifetime, and the harvest is vast. You cannot afford to remain status quo or even to shrink!

Satan's aggressive strategy is snaring millions in his wicked net. We must be equally aggressive with our faith to conquer our cities, our nation, and then the nations of the world. By faith, the saints of old conquered kingdoms (Heb. 11:33), and so must we.

Rise up in faith to conquer! Faith must become your shield, the same shield Abram held that night under the stars of Israel. Once the shield of faith is in place, however, you are ready to advance to what brings the victory: spiritual warfare.

QUESTIONS TO THINK ABOUT

1. All of us have an area of influence. In this area, we can reach others for Christ and advance God's kingdom. What is your specific area of influence? Who in that circle needs Christ? How could you begin building your faith and releasing it to see God use you as a soulwinner in your area of influence?

2. True faith always includes trust. How can you tell if you are truly trusting God and walking in faith in a certain situation? What is the difference between having faith and trying to work up faith?

3. What is the relationship between your words and your faith? Think of a time when your words built your faith and a time when your words destroyed your faith. What did you learn from those instances?

4. What is the greatest challenge to your faith that you ever faced? How did you keep yourself spiritually strong in the trial? What happened to your faith as a result of the trial?

5. What vision has God given you for which you need faith in order to see its fulfillment? What are you doing to develop your faith in your vision?

CHAPTER 14

COMMANDMENT 9: SPIRITUAL WARFARE

For we do not wrestle against flesh and blood, but against principalities, against powers, against the rulers of the darkness of this age, against spiritual hosts of wickedness in the heavenly places.

—EPHESIANS 6:12, NKJV

A YOUNG PASTOR STRUGGLING WITH CHURCH power issues once asked my father, "In your sixty years of ministry, what is the number one lesson you have learned?" Pausing for a moment, my father answered, "People are not your enemy."

That simple phrase embodies the thought of the ninth commandment of ministry. If you fail to see behind the movements and manipulations of people and into the spirit world of darkness, you will fight the wrong enemy.

A friend of mine was a Golden Gloves champion fighter. In one bout, he was taking a real beating. His coach tried to cheer him up by saying, "Get in there, champ; he hasn't laid a glove on you yet." Looking through the blood coming from his eye, my friend said to his coach, "Would you please keep your eye on the referee, then?" He knew he was getting hit, but he didn't know where it was coming from!

We believers face the same predicament. Our families, emotions, health, finances, and ministries all seem to be challenged at once. But Christians sometimes have the strange thought that if they are in the will of God, they will never encounter the devil. If that were true, then Paul must have been out of the will of God most of the time.

If you never run into the devil, you must be going in his direction! But if you get close to something the enemy does not want to give up, you can expect him to draw his big guns against you. Like a team defending its goal against the final score, the enemy goes into a goal-line stand when you actually threaten him.

Someone said, "Big demons guard big treasures." Satan guards certain areas of deception, murder, immorality, strife, government, and many other key areas. For most people, he simply sets a little demon on the roof of their house and says, "If they ever wake up, come get me." But a Christian who clearly sees the principle of spiritual warfare becomes a clear and present danger to the enemy.

I first discovered this principle as a missionary in Ghana, West Africa. Melanie and I had been married for only two weeks when we arrived at the mission station. Along with the rest of the team, we ministered in areas around Lake Volta, where there was no gospel witness, and openly challenged the witch doctors. For six months, we saw the reality of the powers of darkness as our little band of nine missionaries suffered repeated attack, spiritually, physically, and emotionally. One young lady from Germany even lost her mind and had to be taken home in a straitjacket.

One night I had a horrific dream of a person telling me to go home. As I resisted the person in the dream, I woke up to see a shimmering white object at the foot of my bed. I felt as if this "thing" had pinned my lips back to my ears, and I felt like I was dying. However, my spirit rose up within me as the name *Jesus* seemed to float up and out of my mouth. The demonic presence left the room instantly.

Having just graduated from college with a theological and historical degree, I was not prepared for a manifestation such as that. But it proved to me the reality of my enemy and enabled me to continue our work in Ghana and Nigeria over a period of almost two years (three terms of six months). In those areas of the world, theory about spiritual warfare is irrelevant because reality is so obvious.

When I returned to the States, the spiritual environment was so easy compared to West Africa that it felt as though I was running on asphalt instead of in sand. But while I was in Africa, the demonic oppression, confusion, and discouragement were almost tangible on a daily basis.

Those who deny the reality of spiritual warfare generally have limited experience in other cultures where the gospel has not penetrated. I once visited the Muslim stronghold of Lamu Island off the coast of Kenya. This fifteen-hundred-year-old stronghold is a training ground for the imams of East Africa. Strolling down the street one day, I became aware of how difficult it was to even walk straight or grasp a clear thought. I have never felt the presence of such demonic realities as I did on that island.

Paul dealt with spiritual warfare in his first encounter with a sorcerer (Acts 13:8), with the girl with a familiar spirit at Philippi (Acts 16:16), and with the demonic powers at Ephesus (Acts 19:12). He told the Thessalonians, "We wanted to come to you—I, Paul, more than once—and yet Satan hindered us" (1 Thess. 2:18). If Paul faced demonic opposition, you can be sure you will face it as well.

The question is, do you recognize it for what it is? Jesus said to Peter, "Get behind Me, Satan!" (Matt. 16:23), because He recognized the voice of the enemy using Peter's intellect. When you realize that Satan may be using someone as a tool, you stop fighting the person and start fighting the enemy. In prayer, you can "resist the devil and he will flee from you" (James 4:7). But how easy it is to slip back into the natural mentality and allow Satan to escape unnoticed while we slug it out with one another!

This does not in any way diminish or excuse poor character, nor does it say that all opposition is demonic. You may need to hear another opinion if yours is wrong. However, an individual who exhibits constant friction, strife, confusion, and undermining is being used as a tool in the enemy's hands. In your private prayer time, you can bind the enemy that is using the person, while continuing to love the individual.

COVERING IN WARFARE

David said, "You have covered my head in the day of battle" (Ps. 140:7). A covering is a shield of protection, a wall of defense, and spiritual covering is critical to staying strong in spiritual warfare. Of course, the obvious covering for Christians is the armor of God described in Ephesians 6:13–18. Daily in prayer,

I spiritually put on the various parts of the armor: truth, righteousness, peace, faith, salvation, and the Word of God. Although these are obviously figurative attributes of God, they also represent real defenses we need in place over our hearts and minds.

Isn't it interesting that the armor starts with *truth*? Any deception creates a chink in your armor, but with honesty and transparency intact, you leave no "place to the devil" (Eph. 4:27, NKJV). *Righteousness* over your heart means that you have no sense of guilt, inferiority, or condemnation in your spirit. It is amazing how many believers tolerate a sense of being second-rate spiritually.

Peace over your feet means that you will walk in a sense of order and direction (not chaos and confusion). *Salvation* as a helmet protects your thoughts and keeps discouragement, fear, lust, and a host of other suggestions from lodging in your mind. *Faith* is your shield (see the previous chapter) so that you can stand in confidence and relaxation that everything is going to work out regardless of what Satan does. And, finally, just as Jesus had a sharp sword that came out of His mouth in John's vision (Rev. 1:16), you can have God's Word constantly flowing out of your mouth to attack the enemy.

Another area in which to check your covering is your relationship to authority. God's authority provides a shield in life: parents for children, husbands for wives, pastors for sheep. When we move into rebellion, however, we give Satan a legal "argument" to be present, and no amount of spiritual warfare will move him.

Miriam and Aaron learned that speaking against godly, legitimate authority is dangerous, even to your health (Num. 12:10).

They had to learn the hard way the truth of what I have taught earlier in this book: everyone needs spiritual accountability.

Accountability is necessary in marriage too. Ruth said to Boaz, "Spread your covering over your maid" (Ruth 3:9). A godly wife longs to be in proper relationship to her husband in spiritual authority. Of course, he is to cover her, not smother her. The husband's role is actually much like that of a police officer's relationship with the public. Both provide security and protection but never invade your privacy unauthorized.

Conquering in Warfare

Paul wrote about spiritual conquest in 2 Corinthians 10:3–5: "For though we walk in the flesh, we do not war according to the flesh, for the weapons of our warfare are not of the flesh, but divinely powerful for the destruction of fortresses. We are destroying speculations and every lofty thing raised up against the knowledge of God, and we are taking every thought captive to the obedience of Christ."

Satan's attacks are often devious and subtle. In chapter 9, I discussed in detail the processes involved in the progression of sin from a thought to an action. Suffice it to say that at each level, you must actively resist, or you are in grave danger of being ensnared in greater and greater levels of sin and bondage.

James Robison has described how a stronghold of lust gradually worked its way into his mind over the course of years. He said it was like a claw in his brain. Although happily married, he found himself struggling with lust and toying with ideas of other women. One day, however, God used a carpet cleaner

who worked for James to set him free, and now God uses James
mightily to set other Christians free.[1]

*The initial thought is the most dangerous stage in any temp-
tation.* If you don't stop a thought, it will escalate and you'll take
it in as truth. As you dwell on the "truth," eventually you take
an action based upon the lie you have believed. The first illicit
touch, the first lustful look, or the first thing hidden boosts
your thought processes a notch higher: "How good this tastes!
How restrictive were my old ideas!" You have now pierced the
veil of taboo and tasted the forbidden. Now you begin plotting
how to cover up your sin and continue in it.

When you fail to recognize the enemy's tactics and thus fail
to go into battle against him, sin enters your life and, if not
dealt with, eventually becomes a pattern of behavior. It can be
something truly horrible or something as simple as fear. But
the point is, it is a bondage.

A friend of mine once had a dream in which a demonic
power sat on a throne in a room. A man seemed glued to the
throne this demon was sitting on. My friend felt himself being
pulled into the same position and said in the dream, "You will
never get me there," and walked out. A short while later, my
friend, who traveled extensively, began to experience a fear
of flying. Eventually it got to the point where he would only
drive to engagements. This went on for over a year as his initial
thought became a fortress in his mind.

As he prayed one day, the Lord reminded him of his dream
and showed him that he, indeed, had been overpowered. He
prayed for release and then booked a round-trip flight from
his hometown to another city two hundred miles away. He

successfully completed the trip and remained free of that fear the rest of his life.

COURAGE IN WARFARE

The Book of Joshua is our template for warfare. It begins with an admonition from the Lord to Joshua, repeated three times in rapid succession: "Be strong and courageous" (Josh. 1:6–7, 9). The word *courage* comes from a French word *couer*, which means "heart." Thus, to *have courage* is to "take heart."

Satan does not play fair. He is a bully who progresses through fear. I heard a story once of a bully on a playground who kept the entire school trembling in fear. A frail, skinny adolescent walked up beside him one day and noticed a list in his hand. "What's that?" he questioned the bully. "A list of everyone on this playground that I can beat up," the bully answered. The slight boy noticed his name on the list, but refusing to be intimidated, he faced the bully and shrieked, "You can't beat me up!" The bully immediately turned his pencil over and erased the other boy's name!

You cannot sit around and analyze *why* and *how* when dealing with the enemy. You must have courage. Your heart cannot become faint in the battle. Satan will bluff and use any tactic, including intimidation, lies, or fear, to try to force you to back down. But you must recognize his tactics and command him to desist in his maneuvers. Moses did not back down from Korah (Num. 16), Peter did not back down from Simon (Acts 8), Paul did not back down from Elymas (Acts 13), and you must not back down from the enemy!

Perhaps today you are walking into a spiritual storm. Rise up as Jesus did on the boat with His disciples. Mark records,

"There arose a fierce gale" (Mark 4:37). Right after that, it says, "Then He arose and rebuked the wind" (v. 39, NKJV). When the wind arose, He arose!

This wind was nothing but a demonic resistance trying to keep Jesus from crossing the sea and delivering the demoniac. It was obviously not from God, or Christ would not have rebuked it. The point is, when demonic opposition arises, you also must arise. Solidly plant your feet on biblical grounds and "stand your ground" (Eph. 6:13, NIV). The weapons you fight with are not fleshly but "mighty in God for pulling down strongholds" (2 Cor. 10:4, NKJV). Those mighty weapons include the name of Jesus and the blood of Jesus (Rev. 12:11).

Take possession of your territory the way Joshua did. Take the fight to the enemy before he can attack! Break through his barriers, pull down his thoughts, and release God's power into every area of your life.

Yes, this is real warfare, but it is fought in wisdom by those who have experienced the reality of the conflict. In fact, spiritual warfare and wisdom go hand in hand, and wisdom is the final pillar in the Ten Commandments of Ministry.

QUESTIONS TO THINK ABOUT

1. What does it mean to understand that people are not your enemies? How can grasping this fact help you in your personal relationships?

2. What happens if you don't recognize the devil's subtle tactics against you? What makes it so difficult to recognize his workings?

3. Have you ever known Christians who fear to engage in combat with the devil or his demons? How can they overcome this fear and realize their strength as spiritual warriors?

4. Which part of the armor of God, as listed in Ephesians 6:13–18, do you find yourself relying upon more than any other part? What makes this such a valuable weapon for you?

5. If the devil's power is already broken, why do we still live with his evil effects in our lives? Is there an area of your life in which you need to rise up in faith and engage in spiritual warfare? Will you do it?

CHAPTER 15

COMMANDMENT 10: WISDOM

Wisdom has built her house, she has hewn out her seven pillars.

—PROVERBS 9:1

WISDOM, THE FINAL COMMANDMENT OF THE Ten Commandments of Ministry, should perhaps be the first. Wisdom is truly the principal thing in all of Christian life and ministry and embodies all the other nine commandments.

Laying the foundation and building the structure of any spiritual house require great wisdom and skill. In building his empire, Solomon discovered seven pillars, or facets, of wisdom that were necessary. In the New Testament, Paul called himself a "wise master builder" (1 Cor. 3:10), and Jesus said that a wise man builds his house on a rock (Matt. 7:24).

I have seen many ministries, and even individual Christians, spring up and flourish for a season, but because of a lack of wisdom, they were not sustainable and ultimately failed. But a brief review of Solomon's early days (before pride, greed, and lust captured his heart) will reveal the seven characteristics of wisdom that his kingdom displayed and we need.

THE HEART OF WISDOM

"Now, O LORD my God, You have made Your servant king in place of my father David, yet I am but a little child; I do not know how to go out or come in. Your servant is in the midst of Your people which You have chosen, a great people who are too many to be numbered or counted. So give Your servant an understanding heart to judge Your people to discern between good and evil. For who is able to judge this great people of Yours?" (1 Kings 3:7–9).

Notice in this passage that Solomon asked first for an understanding heart, humbly professing that he was but a child. This illustrates the first quality of wisdom: a meek and humble heart. In essence, Solomon said, "I am in over my head. I don't know what I'm doing. I have no experience here. H-ee-ll-pp!"

I can relate to that, and perhaps you can too. When I became senior pastor of our church at thirty years of age, I felt inadequate to handle tough situations. Of course, I had the benefit of my father's guiding wisdom (and still do), but still, I constantly felt the sense of being out of my league.

Albert Schweitzer said, "Experience is not the best teacher; it's the only teacher." In those early years of ministry, I had little experience and knew it. But the Lord gave me a verse that I memorized and have used constantly for the last twenty-five years: "But the wisdom that is from above is first pure, then peaceable, gentle, willing to yield, full of mercy and good fruits, without partiality and without hypocrisy" (James 3:17, NKJV).

In other words, wisdom is a heart attitude, a humble dependence on God to give you the wisdom you don't have in yourself. Daniel faced that when Nebuchadnezzar demanded that he know *both* his dream and the interpretation of it. In one night, however, God graciously revealed to Daniel these mysteries and saved his life (Dan. 2:19–23).

A humble, childlike heart will always be rewarded with wisdom. But those who are proud, self-assured, and arrogant will stumble from adviser to adviser while committing major blunders. In essence, then, all wisdom starts here—with humility.

THE WORD OF WISDOM

Solomon's first big test of wisdom concerned two prostitutes and one baby (1 Kings 3:16–28). Each woman claimed the baby as her own. If you recall, Solomon's word to cut the baby in half brought instant clarity, as the true mother cried out for the baby's life to be spared.

This is the second pillar of wisdom: God will give you a word of wisdom that will bring instant clarity and closure to a difficult problem. The word of wisdom is listed as the first of the gifts of the Spirit in 1 Corinthians 12:8 and is critical in the solving of difficult problems. Daniel received a word for Nebuchadnezzar, Joseph received a word for Pharaoh, and you too will receive a word when you need it.

As a member of Dr. Yonggi Cho's board for many years, I have heard him share numerous times how God gave him a word of wisdom as he built the world's largest church. Once, his massive auditorium project on Yoido Island came to a standstill because of a lack of funds. Dr. Cho cried out to God for help because no bank would loan him money. In prayer, he received a word to approach a certain bank about a loan. He told the bank that tens of thousands of his church members would very likely shift their accounts in return for the bank helping their church get a loan. Immediately, the bank had a change of heart, loaned Dr. Cho the money, and the building was finished.

When my father began our church in 1964, he did not have all the funds to secure the purchase of the three-acre piece of property and house. As he stood before the banker, my father sensed in his heart the word *subdivide*. Obeying that word, he proposed that the bank subdivide the property, allowing him to buy the house while the new church (zero members) bought the other acreage. The bank agreed, and the rest is history! One word from God entirely solved my father's problem.

Jesus consistently had a word of wisdom when challenged by the Pharisees. Whether it was about taxes, divorce, or the resurrection, He was never confused but knew exactly what to say. In every dilemma you face, God has a word from the Spirit He will drop into your heart.

THE TEAM OF WISDOM

Wisdom can spot, select, and develop a group of people into a winning team. Solomon knew this and "had twelve deputies over all Israel, who provided for the king and his household; each man had to provide for a month in the year" (1 Kings 4:7). Nineteen verses of this chapter in 1 Kings talk about all the people Solomon surrounded himself with. His amazing teams built the temple and coordinated his vast resources. Because of them, his military might was so invincible it was never challenged, and his international trade made him the wealthiest man in the world. All that happened because of the team God helped him to assemble. Solomon knew where his strength came from, saying, "He who walks with wise men will be wise" (Prov. 13:20).

The Southeastern Conference football teams generally concentrate on recruiting players based on speed. However, one losing program in that conference had only one player who could run the forty-yard dash in under 4.5 seconds, while the leading schools boasted twenty! This struggling school then began to recruit for speed instead of experience and soon possessed one of the league's leading programs. The moral of that illustration is this: recruit the "horses" and you will run.

In his famous book *The Master Plan of Evangelism*, Dr. Robert Coleman outlines the eight steps of Jesus's developing His team. He selected them, He confronted them, He developed them, and He released them. He could see the potential within each one of them. He loved them enough to challenge them, and when He finished, He left the entire future of the gospel in their hands.[1]

Paul too developed a team. He had up to fifteen young men who traveled with him constantly: Timothy, Titus, Gaius, Secundus, Luke, and others. He sent them on missions and admonished them to fulfill their ministries. He planted churches that they then pastored and moved them in and out of established churches as his representative.

Being part of a team and then leading a team of your own is not reserved to the clergy. Every Christian believer has the potential to influence someone. You may not know everything about following Christ, but you have learned some things and can transmit that to others. Christianity is not a solo sport; it is a team activity where we share wins and losses, strategies and plans, and lessons learned. We are all teammates answering to the same coach—the Lord Jesus Himself.

Teamwork takes wisdom, but it is the single most important facet of a Christian's long-term success. As Jesus said in Luke 7:35, "Wisdom is justified by all her children" (NKJV). I can promise you that you will move no further than the team you are part of.

The fact that flocks of geese fly farther and faster than a lone goose reveals nature's built-in understanding of the value of teamwork. It's the same in the spiritual world. The greatest churches in the world possess a strong core leadership who have the utmost respect for the leader, loyalty to the vision, and drive to accomplish it. Nothing can stop a great team!

THE BLESSING OF WISDOM

"Judah and Israel were as numerous as the sand that is on the seashore in abundance; they were eating and drinking and rejoicing" (1 Kings 4:20). Solomon's team produced abundance, and they obviously understood how to handle finances well. Managing money wisely is a skill God rewards. But many churches and individual Christians seek greater blessing instead of greater wisdom in stewardship. God supplies our needs, but we often lack the wisdom to maximize His provision.

I did not earn an MBA in college and had to learn the hard way about budgets, human resources, indebtedness, construction, and the myriad of administrative skills needed to successfully lead a large ministry. I had to ask the Lord for wisdom.

Satan is a master at keeping us ignorant of the simplest principles of God's blessing. God does not bless ignorance. He rewards the stewards who are productive and long-sighted. He blesses those who take care of the poor.

A missionary friend of ours in Kenya told a most interesting story about a man in Kenya who wanted to support her ministry. He owned an oil-recycling business, and one day he noticed a leak at an oil refinery that he serviced. The leak was being caught in barrels, as the company said it would cost too much to shut down the refinery and fix the leak. The man asked if he could have the leaked material if he would haul it off. The refinery agreed, and this man, over time, sold the leaked oil for enough money to build a huge retreat facility for our friend's ministry. If God can do that with nothing more than a "drip," imagine what He can do through you as you wisely use the resources He has entrusted to you!

Of course, we know that generous giving changes the degree of blessing. A missionary friend of mine in Haiti learned that very few church members in that country tithed. He, however, required all his pastors to tithe (even vegetables, if they had no money), and suddenly their churches' finances began to turn around. Soon members were prospering (comparatively in Haitian standards) far above other congregations in the same area.

It requires finances to purchase, construct, and maintain facilities for people to grow together and in Christ. It takes dollars for a family to afford an adequate house, send their children to school, and still have resources to invest in the kingdom. But a person with wisdom can take a sum of money and produce far more with it than can someone else who lacks wisdom. Wisdom will motivate the first person to save rather than waste money, while the second person does not have that restraint.

Solomon enjoyed favor with surrounding nations, and his wealth was legendary. We know that we cannot measure spirituality simply by spreadsheets, because prosperity is relative to culture. However, Satan is the author of financial bondage, and we need God's wisdom in order to see through his temptations and snares of financial foolishness.

THE PEACE OF WISDOM

"And he [Solomon] had peace on all sides around about him. So Judah and Israel lived in safety, every man under his vine and his fig tree, from Dan even to Beersheba, all the days of Solomon" (1 Kings 4:24–25). Peace results from order. Because Solomon had both the finances and the affairs of the kingdom in order, the entire nation lived in peace.

Confusion, the opposite of order, is not of God. Many people, however, live in a constant state of confusion. Lack of planning, punctuality, provision, and purpose leads to continual upheaval. Last-minute decisions and communication keep everyone in flux. These results of confusion are true whether in a family, a ministry, or a nation.

Wisdom, on the other hand, produces peace: "The wisdom from above is first pure, then peaceable" (James 3:17). Because of Solomon's order and wisdom, Israel lived in a sense of protection and well-being. Forty thousand horses and a large army discouraged any potential invaders, and peace was the rule of the day.

When there is upheaval in church government, turmoil over growth decisions, disagreements over choir specials, unchecked "staff" infection, or unrest in any of the other hundreds of confusion possibilities in a church, the atmosphere becomes hostile and tense. Visitors and members alike can sense the dysfunction and will take steps to remove their families from it.

Sheep graze and breed in an environment of peace. Still waters make them lie down. But where there is no order, everyone is edgy. It's like the gas gauge in your car. If the gauge is broken, you remain on edge, not knowing whether you are about to run out of gas. A properly functioning gas gauge, however, brings you peace, because you know exactly where you stand at any given moment.

Our lives are surrounded by situations that can steal our peace, and most of them deal with order. Paul told the Corinthians, "God is not a God of confusion but of peace.... But all things must be done properly and in an orderly manner" (1 Cor. 14:33, 40). When there is a swirl of confusion, panic, missed deadlines, cancellations, no contingency planning, and miscommunications, you can be certain that the Spirit of peace is not present.

Choose to miss "golden opportunities" if they bring confusion, complexity, and misunderstanding. You will be trusted as wise and stable if you make steady, well-thought-out, simple-to-communicate directional moves instead of jerky, unplanned actions. Think of your life like the *Queen Elizabeth* (with a twenty-five-mile turning radius) rather than a speedboat (twenty-five-foot turning radius). Let others follow every new fad, while you remain consistent and conservative. The peace your life generates will be tangible!

I will never forget an unsaved contractor telling me how he had passed our building on the highway, glanced over at our property, and, in his words, "peace hit him in the face." This gentleman turned his car around in the median, marched into the building, surrendered his heart to the Lord, and remained a strong member of the church before eventually moving out of state. That same kind of peace surrounded Solomon's entire kingdom, and God wants it to surround your life and ministry too.

THE CREATIVITY OF WISDOM

> Now God gave Solomon wisdom and very great discernment and breadth of mind, like the sand that is on the seashore. Solomon's wisdom surpassed the wisdom of all the sons of the east and all the wisdom of Egypt. For he was wiser than all men, than Ethan the Ezrahite, Heman, Calcol and Darda, the sons of Mahol; and his fame was known in all the surrounding nations. He also spoke 3,000 proverbs, and his songs were 1,005. He spoke of trees, from the cedar that is in Lebanon even to the hyssop that grows on the wall; he spoke also of animals and birds and creeping things and fish.
>
> —1 KINGS 4:29–33

Most people copy rather than create, and we Christians are no different. Running from conference to conference, we are quick to grab on to things that the people presenting them are no longer doing! There is certainly nothing wrong with copying others, but God is a God of endless variety. Solomon spoke of things no one else had ever dreamed of. His metaphors and proverbs, songs and poems, and botanical and zoological wisdom were unending. Jesus too moved in this creative wisdom. He told parables that remain unmatched in their ability to make complex truths simple.

In the corporate world, the creative rule the day. When creating their iPhone, Apple held two hundred patents—and we in the church sit and study one another! All too often, it's as Jesus said: "For the sons of this world are for their own generation wiser than the sons of the light" (Luke 16:8, ASV). On the other hand, one of Solomon's proverbs said, "He who wins souls is wise" (Prov. 11:30, NIV), and there should be creative, fresh ideas from the Holy Spirit to accomplish the great task of soul-winning.

Solomon's wisdom extended into the realm of the arts (music), literature (poetry and proverbs), and science (botany, zoology, ornithology), and he had "breadth of mind, like the sand that is on the seashore" (1 Kings 4:29). Ask the Holy Spirit to release within your heart a spirit of creativity to present the gospel in fresh, powerful ways to your particular culture and demographic. Through music, message, and practical wisdom, make the gospel "salty" and irresistible to those in your culture struggling for answers.

Using what others are doing is acceptable, but it is not the limit. God has embedded a unique fingerprint on your hand and assigned a distinctive signature to your personality. When you allow that unique flow of creativity to be released, you allow the final pillar of wisdom to be erected in your life.

THE PROMOTION OF WISDOM

"Men came from all peoples to hear the wisdom of Solomon, from all the kings of the earth who had heard of his wisdom" (1 Kings 4:34). Wisdom will promote you; that is why it must begin with humility. People from everywhere came to hear the wisdom of Solomon. His wisdom far excelled the men of the East, those whose intellects had given them great reputation. When you are able to solve the problems of people in the world, they will seek you as a fountain of wisdom.

I heard once of a man whose company awarded him a beautiful office complete with a rocking chair and a picture window. All day long, all this man did was sit in his chair and gaze out the window. Some of the other employees grew disgruntled at his seeming lack of work. They complained to the manager, who replied, "Last year that man solved a problem that saved us millions of dollars, so we gave him whatever he asked for!"

You are valuable to God and possess the potential of amazing creativity, growth, and development. God promoted Joseph, Daniel, Nehemiah, and a host of other leaders in Scripture, and His every intention is to promote your influence as well.

You must never seek promotion, but always lay all the glory at the feet of Christ. However, at the same time, you will not be able to stop it as you move in the *heart*, the *word*, the *team*, the *prosperity*, the *peace*, and the *creativity* of wisdom. Solomon also recognized this powerful principle: "Wisdom is the principal thing; therefore get wisdom. And in all your getting, get understanding. Exalt her, and she will promote you; she will bring you honor, when you embrace her. She will place on your head an ornament of grace; a crown of glory she will deliver to you" (Prov. 4:7–9, NKJV).

It is fitting that our Ten Commandments of Ministry conclude with this powerful principle of wisdom. In essence, all of the other nine are encompassed in it. Seek wisdom as the "principal thing." Claim the mind of Christ in all ten areas of ministry.

Purpose that you will become a model of Christ's wisdom

to the dark world around you. They have seen the biggest and the greatest fall. Sadly, they have ridiculed the tenets of Christ because of the church's example. We know that we are not perfect, but we can "conduct [ourselves] with wisdom toward outsiders, making the most of the opportunity" (Col. 4:5).

I see a new generation of Christians rising up, determined not to repeat the mistakes of the past. We cannot undo our mistakes, but we must learn from them. We must set a standard of holiness, ethics, purity, and wisdom that makes the world envious and hungry for Jesus. The wisdom of these Ten Commandments of Ministry should naturally evolve into a fresh yet timeless code of conduct that we pledge our lives, our families, and our ministries to uphold.

QUESTIONS TO THINK ABOUT

1. Think about the wisest person you know. Is that person also a humble person? Why is it not possible to have true wisdom without true humility?

2. How would you define the word of wisdom as a gift of the Holy Spirit? Have you ever given or received a supernatural word of wisdom? What was it, and how did it help you? How was it different from natural wisdom?

3. What does it mean to be led by your peace? Why is this a wise way to help you make difficult decisions? Think of a time when you followed your peace and another time when you failed to follow your peace. What happened in each case, and what did you learn?

4. How does God's wisdom make you more creative? What is the most original, creative idea you ever had, and how did you know it was from God? How do we sometimes stifle God's creative flow?

5. Promotion comes from the hand of the Lord, not from man (although we can push ourselves forward). What is the difference between God's promotion and our efforts to promote ourselves? When promotion does come, what is the proper response? Have you ever seen someone receive promotion from the Lord but be unable to handle it because of pride? What happened to cause the person to stumble, and how could it have been avoided?

A Personal Code
of Conduct

T HE PRECEDING FIFTEEN CHAPTERS ARE A STARTING point for turning around the ministry in America, both in a church and in an individual Christian. Volumes could be written on each subject, but the general must come down to the specific.

It's difficult to quantify a code of conduct for believers to live by. However, for the sake of changing our nation, I will dive into this as a "long beginning" intended to end in national revival in the American church. The following ten points are a basic commitment to live by the Ten Commandments of Ministry as explained in this book:

1. I pledge myself to a life of *prayer and fasting,* making time alone with God my highest priority (Acts 6:4).
2. I pledge myself to faithfully study, teach, preach, and apply the *Scripture* itself (2 Tim. 3:1–4:4).

3. I pledge myself to *integrity* in the areas of financial accountability, commitments, honesty, and doctrine (Heb. 13:18).

4. I pledge myself to moral *purity* in thoughts, media, appearances, and the marriage covenant (Heb. 13:4).

5. I pledge myself to be an *example* in my work habits, community reputation, and family model (1 Tim. 3:1–7).

6. I pledge myself to covenant *relationships* that foster accountability, networking, team building, and a kingdom mentality (Heb. 13:17).

7. I pledge myself to a *philosophy* of simplicity, sincerity, and sacrifice (2 Cor. 1:12).

8. I pledge myself to living a life of *faith* through clear vision, fearless trust, and a conquering mentality (1 Tim. 6:12).

9. I pledge myself to *spiritual warfare* against principalities, not people (2 Cor. 10:1–5).

10. I pledge myself to walk in the humility, teamwork, order, and creativity of *wisdom* (Eph. 5:15).

Though certainly not all-inclusive, these ten commitments form a good foundation on which to base a solid, fruitful, life-long ministry. As the culture of America grows ever darker, I challenge all of you to "prove yourselves to be blameless and innocent, children of God above reproach in the midst of a crooked and perverse generation, among whom you appear as lights in the world" (Phil. 2:15). *You can help change the nation if you will first change yourself.*

I pray God's richest blessings upon you for taking the time to read and study these simple, foundational truths. Pastor by pastor, leader by leader, believer by believer, a new brand of Christian will emerge, "blameless," "innocent," and "above reproach." Purpose from this moment forward that you will make your highest aim to be a part of *the remnant*!

NOTES

CHAPTER 1
MENTORING FOR THE UNFATHERED CHURCH

1. John Eldredge, *Wild at Heart* (Nashville: Thomas Nelson, Inc., 2001), 65–70.

2. Ibid., 108–115.

CHAPTER 2
STANDARDS FOR THE UNCORRECTED CHURCH

1. Henry Cloud and John Townsend, *Boundaries with Kids* (Grand Rapids, MI: Zondervan, 1998), 64.

2. Ibid., 65–67.

3. Ibid., 58–61.

CHAPTER 3
MULTIPLICATION FOR THE UNFRUITFUL CHURCH

1. Bill Bright, *5 Steps to Making Disciples* (Orlando: New Life Publications, 1997), 7–8.

CHAPTER 5
THE SCRIPTURES FOR THE UNTAUGHT CHURCH

1. George Bush Presidential Library and Museum, "Public Papers—1990," http://bushlibrary.tamu.edu/research/public_papers.php?id=2582&year=1990&month=all (accessed June 18, 2008).

CHAPTER 6
COMMANDMENT 1: PRAYER

1. Dr. David Yonggi Cho of Yoido Full Gospel Church in Seoul, South Korea, has popularized this method of prayer through many avenues of media. I have summarized the method and included some of my own research in this description.

CHAPTER 9
COMMANDMENT 4: PURITY

1. James Dobson, *Love for a Lifetime* (Sisters, OR: Multnomah Books, 1994), 32–34.

CHAPTER 10
COMMANDMENT 5: EXAMPLE

1. John Donne, "Meditation XVII," from *Devotions Upon Emergent Occasions*, viewed at http://isu.indstate.edu/ilnprof/ENG451/ISLAND/text.html (accessed June 19, 2008).

CHAPTER 11
COMMANDMENT 6: RELATIONSHIPS

1. Quotations.com, http://www.quotations.com/wis/3030.htm (accessed June 19, 2008).

2. Robert E. Coleman, *The Master Plan of Evangelism* (Grand Rapids: Fleming H. Revell, a division of Baker Book House Company, 1993).

CHAPTER 12
COMMANDMENT 7: PHILOSOPHY

1. Chip Heath and Dan Heath, *Made to Stick* (New York: Random House, 2007), 33–46.

CHAPTER 14
COMMANDMENT 9: SPIRITUAL WARFARE

1. James Robison, *Knowing God as Father* (Fort Worth, TX: LIFE Outreach International, 1996), 45–50, as viewed at http://www .lifetoday.org/site/DocServer/lifeoutreach__knowing.pdf?docID=142 (accessed June 20, 2008).

CHAPTER 15
COMMANDMENT 10: WISDOM

1. Coleman, *The Master Plan of Evangelism.*

FREE NEWSLETTERS
TO HELP EMPOWER YOUR LIFE

Why subscribe today?

☐ **DELIVERED DIRECTLY TO YOU.** All you have to do is open your inbox and read.

☐ **EXCLUSIVE CONTENT.** We cover the news overlooked by the mainstream press.

☐ **STAY CURRENT.** Find the latest court rulings, revivals, and cultural trends.

☐ **UPDATE OTHERS.** Easy to forward to friends and family with the click of your mouse.

CHOOSE THE E-NEWSLETTER THAT INTERESTS YOU MOST:

- Christian news
- Daily devotionals
- Spiritual empowerment
- And much, much more

SIGN UP AT: **http://freenewsletters.charismamag.com**

8178